AF017

MASSIMILIANO AFIERO

AXIS FORCES
17

WW2 AXIS FORCES

The Axis Forces 017 - First edition March 2021by Luca Cristini Editor for the brand Soldiershop
Cover & Art Design by soldiershop factory.   ISBN code: 978-88-93277358

The Axis Forces number 17 – March 2021

Direction and editing
Via San Giorgio, 11 – 80021 AFRAGOLA (NA) -ITALY

Managing and Chief Editor: Massimiliano Afiero
Email: maxafiero@libero.it - **Website**: www.maxafiero.it

Contributors
Tomasz Borowski, Grégory Bouysse, Stefano Canavassi, Carlos Caballero Jurado, Rene Chavez, Gary Costello, Paolo Crippa, Carlo Cucut, Antonio Guerra, John B. Köser, Lars Larsen, Christophe Leguérandais, Eduardo M. Gil Martínez, Michael D. Miller, Peter Mooney, Péter Mujzer, Ken Niewiarowicz, Erik Norling, Raphael Riccio, Marc Rikmenspoel, Samcevich Andrei, Charles Trang, Cesare Veronesi, Sergio Volpe

Editorial

Hi guys. Still amidst a thousand difficulties and with the global pandemic present, we managed to finish this new issue of our magazine, hoping to have always done our best and to have made interesting articles for all our readers. In this last period, many articles by historians, students and simple enthusiasts have been reaching us from every corner of the world, eager to see their works published in our magazine. Articles on the battles, the campaigns of the Second World War, but also stories of units and biographies of fighters. We will try to please everyone, as far as possible. However, we invite everyone to focus more on the voluntary Axis formations, those made up of foreign volunteers and integrated in the German, Italian and Japanese armies. It is precisely on the war in the Pacific that we want to make a few more articles in particular. While waiting for your comments and recommendations, let's now analyze the contents of this new issue: let's start with the formation of the SS Division Nord *in 1941, on the eve of its employment on the Finnish front. Following is the biography of* Josef Rollecke, *a man decorated with the Knight's Cross, of the 3. SS-Panzer Division 'Totenkopf'. We continue with the first part of an in-depth study on the history of* Frikorps Danmark, *the Danish volunteer formation. Another biography dedicated to* Georg Keppler, *commanding officer of the Waffen-SS follows. The study dedicated to Italians decorated with the Iron Cross is certainly interesting and we close with the fifth and last part of the article dedicated to the employment of the* Cossacks *in the German armed forces. Happy reading everyone and see you at the next issue.*

Massimiliano Afiero

Contents

in World War Two 1939-1945

Formation of the SS-Division 'Nord'
by Massimiliano Afiero

A *Sturmmann* of an *SS-Totenkopfverband.*

SS-Hstuf. Walter Jurk of the *SS-Inf.Rgt.6.*

The *"Nord"* Division was formed based mainly on two *SS-Totenkopf-Standarten, SS-Totenkpf-Standarte 6* and *7*, which had been deployed to Norway since 1940 as occupation forces, and to which for a brief time *SS-Totenkopf-Standarte 9 "Kirkenes"* was also attached. These units in turn traced their origins to the *SS-Totenkopfverbände*, created initially to serve in the German concentration camps, which by a decree signed by Hitler on May 18, 1939 had been transformed into units to be employed in the front lines. Thanks to the same decree the *Reichsführer-SS*, Heinrich Himmler, was authorized to expand the force of the *SS-Totenkopfverbände*, and before the war began he began forming new *SS-Totenkopf-Standarten*, recruiting members of the *Allgemeine-SS*, police reservists and diverting many young volunteers from mandatory conscription. Members of the *SS-Totenkopf-Standarten* were also authorized to wear the *feldgrau* uniform, as were all of the *Waffen-SS* combatants. According to Himmler's plans, these units would be used as occupation forces and as police forces in occupied territory.

SS-Kampfgruppe Nord

In February 1941, *SS-Totenkopf-Standarte 6* and *7* were transferred to Norwegian Lapland, in the Kirkenes area; on February 24, an order issued by the *SS-FHA* authorized the formation of *SS-Kampfgruppe Nord*, grouping the two SS regiments and a signals detachment together. The same order authorized the formation of other units to be integrated into the *Kampfgruppe* by March 15; a headquarters, a map section, two engineer companies, a reconnaissance battalion and other minor service units.

SS-Brigdf. **Richard Herrmann.**

Movement of SS units, 1940-1941.

SS-Inf.Rgt.7 **troops on the Finnish front.**

On February 25, to lend a greater military aspect to this new combat group and to render it to all intents and purposes a *Waffen SS* combat formation, the two *Standarten*, were officially redesignated as *SS-Infanterie-Regiment 6* and *7*. This transformation was in line with Himmler's project, begun in the autumn of 1940, to expand his *Waffen SS*, using the human resources of the *SS-Totenkopf-Standarten*. Command of *SS-Kampfgruppe Nord* was initially assigned to *SS-Brigdf.* Richard Herrmann. Training of the unit met with delays because his units were engaged in patrolling the coast between Kirkenes and Vardö, where there were fears of possible Allied landings and raids. The German units deployed in Lapland were there to defend the valuable Norwegian mines but were also awaiting the imminent offensive on the Eastern Front. In fact it was from Lapland that the German offensive against Murmansk and the Kola Peninsula was to originate. On June 8, 1941 the units received the order to reach the Ranua-Rovaniemi sector in Finland. The *Kampfgruppe* was moved by train as far as Mosjön, where it was embarked upon Norwegian vessels to Billefjord. One of the ships, the *Blenheim*, was sabotaged by the Norwegian resistance and a hundred and ten men of *SS-Inf.Rgt.6*, among them twenty-four personnel of the *Vorkommando* (the advance headquarters, sent to the operational sector beforehand to arrange for the location of the units) of the headquarters, lost their lives. Shaken by this action, between 7 and 10 June the men of the *Kampfgruppe* reached the Ranua area southeast of Rovaniemi, where they were attached to *XXXVI.Armee-Korps* (*Höheres Kommando z.b.V. XXXVI*) under *General der Infanterie* Hans Feige.

SS-Division Nord

On June 15, 1941, *SS-Brigdf.* Demelhuber assumed command of the unit, bringing with him other staff officers from Germany.

SS-Gruf. Karl Maria Demelhuber.

Training recruits on the *MG-34* machine gun.

The following day, the *Kampfgruppe* received a motorized artillery regiment as reinforcement, consisting of two groups with a total of five light batteries, one heavy battery and a *Flak* battery with 20mm guns. On June 17, 1941 the *Kampfgruppe* was officially established as a new SS division, the *SS-Division "Nord"*, with the following command structure:

<u>Div.Kdr.</u>: *SS-Brigdf.* Demelhuber
<u>Ia</u>: *SS-Ostubaf.* Geisler
<u>Adjutant</u>: *SS-Hstuf.* Schmorell, then *SS-Hstuf.* Kesten
<u>Ic</u>: *SS-Hstuf.* Hans Neumann, then *SS-Hstuf.* Robert Frank
<u>V</u>: *SS-Hstuf.* Wilhelm Ruhl
<u>01</u>: *SS-Hstuf.* Ludwig Weber

<u>SS-Inf.Rgt.6</u>: *SS-Obf.* Voss
I.Bataillon: *SS-Stubaf.* Schreiber
II.Bataillon: *SS-Hstuf.* Elsner
III Bataillon: *SS-Hstuf.* Benner

<u>SS-Inf.Rgt.7</u>: *SS-Staf.* Scheider, then *SS-Ostubaf.* Jens
I.Bataillon: *SS-Hstuf.* Franz Augsberger
II.Bataillon: *SS-Ostubaf.* Schinke, *SS-Ustuf.* Kuhler
III Bataillon: *SS-Stubaf.* Braun

<u>SS-Art.Rgt.</u>: *SS-Ostuf.* Gutberlet
I.Abteilung: *SS-Stubaf.* von Quirsfeld, then *SS-Hstuf.* Klaphake
II.Abteilung: *SS-Stubaf.* Ernst Neumann

<u>SS-Aufkl.Abt</u>: *SS-Hstuf.* Eggert Neumann
<u>SS-Flak-Abteilung</u>: *SS-Hstuf.* Hengstmann
<u>Nachrichtengruppe</u>: *SS-Hstuf.* Hans Rüger
<u>Pionier-Kompanie</u>
<u>Feldpostdienste</u>
<u>Sanitätsdienste</u>
<u>Verwaltungsdienste</u>: *SS-Ostubaf.*

A *Horch Kfz.16* belonging to *Nord* on one of the few passable roads on the Finnish front, with the *Hagal* painted on the front fender (*Charles Trang*).

Members of *SS-Inf.Rgt.7* in a Finnish forest during a pause in training, June 1941 (*Andrea Porro Collection*).

Steinhäuser, then *SS-Stubaf*. Mohr Nachschubdienste: *SS-Staf*. Paul Nostitz, then *SS-Stubaf*. Wilhem Honsell

Officially, *SS-Infanterie-Regiment 9* was initially attached to the division. However, its units were only later attached to *Nord*, and only temporarily. Most of the cadre of the new division were reserve officers, while the soldiers themselves had been trained to be used as policemen rather than for front-line duty. It should be noted that the two SS infantry regiments of the division had originally been *SS-Totenkopf-Standarten*.

The *Hagal Rune* was chosen as the division's insignia, which represented the *"unshakable faith"* of the members of the SS. The Hagal Rune was used in many SS ceremonies to symbolize faith in National Socialism. The symbol had been previously used by *Kampfgruppe Nord*: in fact it had been painted in white on all of the units motor vehicles, as can be seen in period photographs.

The Demelhuber report

A few days before the beginning of the war with the Soviet Union, *SS-Kampfgruppe Nord* had an effective strength of 9,513 men: 306 officers, 1,159 NCOs and 8,048 other ranks. After having reviewed the units on parade, *SS-Brigdf*. Demelhuber was very disappointed with their state of readiness and equipment and on June 17, 1941, sent a report to *Generalleutnant* Feige to inform him of the inadequate training of the men and the lack of adequate equipment. In the report, the commander of *Kampfgruppe Nord* asked for an additional two or three months for training and provision of adequate arms and equipment: *"From a preliminary analysis I have discovered that individual training and the knowledge of combat techniques is poor, while collective training has never been undertaken.*

Nord soldiers training with a Czech machine gun, 1941.

Throwing hand grenade.

Nord soldiers on the Finnish front, Summer 1941.

Most of the higher officers and company commanders are reserve officers who are therefore lacking adequate combat experience…Not even one of the battalion commanders has a sufficient grasp of modern combat tactics…The artillery has not had enough time to train to cooperate with the infantry, and likewise neither the anti-tank detachment nor the mortar crews have ever fired live ammunition. There have never been any combined exercises and the troops are not ready to fight a combined action…Unit mobility is limited thanks to the great variety of vehicles issued…this makes it very difficult to keep spare parts on hand…The division can achieve full operational status only if it has the opportunity to spend another two or three months of perfecting its skills at a good training center".

The situation appeared to be quite disastrous, for example, with respect to armament which came from the ex-Czechoslovak Army and which was not enough to equip all of the units. The greatest shortages were of anti-tank weapons, mortars, artillery pieces and anti-aircraft guns. Made only a few days before Operation *Barbarossa*, Demelhuber's observations and complaints were completely ignored by German higher headquarters.

Bibliography

M. Afiero, *"The 6th Waffen-SS Gebirgs (Mountain) Division Nord"*, Schiffer Publishing
F. Schreiber, *"Kampf unter dem Nordlich"*, Munin Verlag 1969
C.Trang, *"Dictionnaire de la Waffen SS, volume I"*, Editions Heimdal

Josef Rolleke – Knight's Cross holder with the 3. SS-Panzer Division 'Totenkopf'

By Peter Mooney

A signed photo of *SS-Unterscharführer* Josef Rolleke.

Born on the 23 rd of August 1924, he was the son of a stonemason; Rolleke took a three-year apprenticeship in masonary, after his initial schooling. From the 8th of April through to the 28th of September 1942, he served his six-month stint in the *R.A.D.;* he followed that by volunteering for the *Waffen-SS.* There are documents on his file that show he served part of his *R.A.D.* service with the *SS-VT Division,* during May 1942; this may have been why he chose to move there for his military service. There is a May-dated signed declaration from Rolleke to show he was volunteering for the *Waffen-SS.*

At the start of October 1942 he began his service with the *7. Kompanie,* SS-Infantry Regiment 3, *SS-Polizei Division,* but on the 18th of the following month, he had been moved to the *Totenkopf Division.* He was no doubt sent there as one of the replacements for that unit, which had recently returned from their Demjansk mauling; his role was that of driver. His training included the use of the *K98,* the *MG 34, MG 42,* Luger, *MP 40* and Model 24 grenades.

He went into Russia himself in the opening months of 1943, when the challenging battle for Kharkov got underway, serving with the 9. Kompanie, Regiment 1. He was promoted to *SS-Obergrenadier* at the start of April. That was followed by the Kursk offensive, then the Mius front battles. Through all of these, Rolleke proved his worth and quickly accumulated various awards and promotions. The award of the Second Class Iron Cross was made on the 27th of August, with the Tank Assault Badge in Bronze coming at the start of September; the same day that he was moved to the rank of *SS-Sturmmann.* They moved further westwards towards, and onto, the Dnjepr River as 1943 began to come to

SS-Unterscharführer **Josef Rolleke.**

an end. They were pursued westwards and in the last few months of that year, they fought towards Fedorowka and on towards Krivoy Rog. During that fighting, Rolleke added the Close Combat Clasp in Bronze on the 21st of September (for combat days stretching from the 6th of July through to the 12th of August), the First Class Iron Cross on the 21st of October, was promoted to *SS-Unterscharführer* at the start of November, with the Silver Wound Badge coming on the 8th of November; he added the Drivers Badge in Bronze just under one week later!

The Knight's Cross

The pressure on *Totenkopf* continued into 1944 and by late-March, they were fighting near the Balta area. Rolleke's bravery came to the fore once more and following this, on the 16th of May 1944, his Divisional Commander, *SS-Gruppenführer* Hermann Priess, wrote a recommendation for the award of the Knight's Cross. That document covered the following action: '*During the night of the 27.03.1944, the Bolsheviks at Balta succeeded in breaching the left flank of the extraordinarily weakened 9. Kompanie, SS-Panzer-Grenadier-Regiment 5 "Totenkopf", and take control of the sole bridge available for the Battalion command post; the III. / SS-Panzer-Grenadier-Regiment 5 "Totenkopf" had no available elements to clear the bridge. The leader of the III. Battalion messenger squad, SS-*Unterscharführer *Rolleke, was ordered to take 5 men on a scouting party mission to reconnoiter the enemy's strength at the bridge.*

Carrying out his assignment with the greatest of prudence, SS-Unterscharführer *Rolleke recognised a weak spot of the Russians and made the independent decision to take his men on the attack. He worked his way up to a few metres distance from the Russians and suddenly broke into the Bolshevik ranks, with the cries of 'Hurrah'. So surprised were the opponents by this sudden attack, they yielded. In a bold offensive action,* SS-Unterscharführer *Rolleke took advantage of the enemy's surprise and forced the more than 100 Bolsheviks well past our positions and inflicted severe losses on them. In doing so, he managed to free a* Feldwebel *and an* Obergefreiter *of the* Wehrmacht *from Russian captivity.*

26 dead Russians were left on the battleground; 11 were taken prisoner by Rolleke, while a heavy machine-gun, 4 light machine-guns, 9 sub-machine guns and numerous rifles were captured. By opening the bridge, SS-Unterscharführer *Rolleke's bold, independent decision and dashing daredevil nature yielded a crucial success that well exceeded his orders. I ask you to give the Knight's Cross of the Iron Cross to* SS-Unterscharführer *Rolleke, in appreciation of his heroic actions and the connected success.*'

SS-*Uscha*. **Rolleke, on the right, during a ceremony.**

Rolleke was in hospital recovering from wounds, when he received the news of his award of the Knight's Cross; also approved on the 16th of June 1944. The Close Combat Clasp in Silver was awarded in mid-August 1944 (for combat days stretching from the 14th of August through to the 21st of November 1943). From mid-October 1944 through to the 12th of March 1945, he was with the *2. Kompanie / SS-Panzergrenadier* Training and Replacement Battalion 3, based in Ellwangen – Jagst. During that time, he is briefly listed as being attached to *SS-Kompanie 'Heyer'* (commanded by *SS-Hauptsturmführer* Wilhelm Heyer), part of an alarm unit raised in February near the Furstenberg area. He may have been wounded there, as he only spent the two days with them; both days were listed as close combat days (Furstenberg and Hill 38.5). He then returned to the *SS-Panzergrenadier* Training and Replacement Battalion 3 and was still listed there as late as the 14th of April 1945.

Josef Rolleke survived the war and was active in the Knight's Cross holder's association, but apparently not the reunions for the *Totenkopf Division*. The Author managed to meet him face to face, during an unscheduled visit to his home (during the return leg of a trip to fellow *Waffen-SS* Knight's Cross holder Eberhard Heder, who lived not too far from him); he was polite enough to allow me entry into his home and spent a short spell talking to me. A fellow *Totenkopf* soldier who attended every reunion for that unit, had not heard of him, when I discussed my visit, hence the conclusion that he never attended *Totenkopf* reunions. Josef Rolleke died on the 28th of September 2011.

This history is taken from the recently released Volume 5 of the 'Waffen-SS Knights and their Battles' series of books. To obtain your copy, go to www.lahpublishing.com. You can also view the book on our Youtube channel: https://www.youtube.com/watch?v=EbbPi3gkAhI&t=5s, Or email me on: contactus@lahpublishing.com

Bibliography

Face to face conversation and subsequent written correspondence with Herr Rolleke
Waffen-SS Knight's and their Battle – Volume 5: June to August 1944, Peter Mooney. Loyalty and Honour Publishing, 2020

regiment and then as an ordinance officer of the division's chief of staff. The recruitment of Danish volunteers for *Nordland* took place later thanks to the Recruitment Office (*Ergänzungsamt der Waffen-SS Nordsee*) in Copenhagen, headed by *SS-Ustuf.* Rudolf Jensen[2], a *Volksdeutsche*, in close collaboration with Fritz Clausen's DNSAP executives.

Christian Frederik von Schalburg.

Fritz Clausen, leader of DNSAP.

Germanic volunteers in training, 1940.

In this first phase, the volunteers came mainly from openly pro-German circles, aiming at the reconstruction of the Danish army, the preservation of national independence in the new European order and above all to create a genuine and close brotherhood of arms with National Socialist Germany. The DNSAP published a circular to be distributed to the various sections of the Party, dated July 20, 1940, in which they recalled the reasons for enlisting in *Nordland*: "... SS-Standarte Nordland *will help to create a good relationship between the German people and that Danish. SS-Standarte Nordland is not an instrument against the Danish people nor against the Danish state* ". The volunteers were also promised that they could settle in the Reich, without losing their Danish nationality. The propaganda booklet read: "... *The* SS-Standarte Nordland *is a regiment of the* Waffen SS, *made up of volunteers from the Nordic countries. Its creation is a step in the realization of the order of the* Führer, *of May 1940, which aims to ensure the peace of Europe for the next thousand years. The men of the Nordic countries, who love their homeland, will be educated in this regiment in order to later return to their countries of origin as vanguard fighters of the great Germanic ideal and there work to ensure that their peoples as a single group unite in a new European popular brotherhood* ".

Germanic volunteers in the *Nordland* regiment, during training with mimetic uniforms.

Danish volunteer in the *Waffen-SS*.

The requirements for enlisting in this first 'foreign' SS regiment were much stricter than those required for enlistment in the *Frikorps Danmark*. They could enlist: "... *All Danes of Aryan blood, aged between 17 and 40, who had passed the medical examination and without a criminal record*". A minimum height of 170 cm was required, exceptionally 168 cm. These volunteers were the first Danish soldiers to be engaged on the front against the Soviets in June 1941, following the *Wiking* division.

Other Danish volunteers also joined the *Nordwest* regiment. Created with a *Führerbefehl* (order of the Führer) of 3 April 1941, the *Nordwest* was the third SS regiment (after *Nordland* and *Westland*) wanted by Himmler to welcome volunteers of Germanic origin: Flemish, Dutch and Danish.

A volunteer of *Nordwest* regiment.

Germanic volunteers in training, 1940.

The actual formation of the *6th SS Freiwilligen Standarte Nordwest* began on 10 April. *SS-Standartenführer* Otto Reich was designated as commander of the regiment. After an intense recruitment campaign, the regiment's strength came to about 2,500 total strengths: 1,400 Dutch, 805 Flemings and 108 Danes. Volunteer training began first in Hamburg (Langenhorn camp) and then in Radom, Poland. Here, the regiment was divided into two contingents, one predominantly Dutch who was transferred to Krakow and one Flemish which remained in Radom. In Himmler's initial intentions, the *Nordwest* regiment was to be engaged as a security force in northwestern Europe unlike the other SS regiments, which were created for use at the front. As the war loomed on the Eastern front, things changed. The formation of the European Volunteer Legions decreed the dissolution of the unit and the transfer of the volunteers to their respective national contingents.

Since the formation of the *Frikorps Danmark* was only started in the first week of July, on June 23, 1941, Clausen's DNSAP launched a new massive propaganda campaign to encourage the recruitment of the Danes in *Nordland*, now with anti-Communist motives. The very active involvement of the DNSAP in recruiting volunteers for the Waffen-SS represented a great opportunity for the Clausen movement. With the possibility of forming a Danish National Socialist government finally faded, it was decided to somewhat impress the SS commands with the ability of the DNSAP to mobilize volunteers, as an alternative route to power. Incredibly even the social democratic newspaper *'Sozial Demokraten'* supported this campaign and on June 26, 1941, published the following proclamation: "... *Danish compatriots! Enlist to fight against the enemy of the world. Fight for the cause of Finland and Denmark. Join the Nordland regiment!* ".

This reference to Finland was a theme very dear to the Nordic peoples. The criminal Soviet attack on the land of a thousand lakes in December 1939 had aroused horror and indignation in all Scandinavian countries and throughout Europe. Regardless of their ideology, the Danes, Swedes and Norwegians sympathized with Finland: voluntary units were formed in Sweden, Norway and Denmark to fight alongside the Finns.

Erik Scavenius and Adolf Hitler.

DNSAP members with recruitment posters for *Frikorps Danmark* **in Copenhagen, Summer 1941.**

Captain von Schalburg was the inspirer of the Danish Volunteer Corps which, however, did not have time to fully reach Finland, before it capitulated and signed an armistice with the Soviets.

The Frikorps Danmark

With the start of the war on the Eastern front, the Danish military and politicians could not remain indifferent to this new anti-Bolshevik campaign and first of all, the preventive arrest of all communist militants in the country was ordered. On June 26, 1941, the Danish government of Erik Scavenius officially broke off diplomatic relations with the Soviet Union. On that same day, Scavenius himself suggested reconstituting the Danish Expeditionary Force formed already during the Finno-Soviet war. The Danish enthusiasm for this Crusade against Bolshevism was so high that it prompted the government to join the Anti-Comintern Pact on November 25, 1941[3], which other German-occupied countries never did. Adherence to the Pact was practically equivalent to a real declaration of war on the Soviet Union. After the breakdown of diplomatic relations with the USSR, the military circles prepared together with the Danish National Socialists of the DSNAP and the already existing structure for the recruitment in the *Nordland*, to form a Danish voluntary unit for the Eastern front specifying that it should be deal with a unit of the same Danish army. The first applications for enlistment began on June 27. On June 29, in the national press, the news was reported that a Danish Free Corps was being organized, called *Frikorps Danmark*, a unit different from the already existing SS *Nordland* regiment and would be: "*... under the command of Danish officers and non-commissioned officers to fight for the New Europe and for the cause of Denmark, against communism*". On that same day, 8 recruitment offices and 24 information offices for *Frikorps* were already active in Denmark. On 2 July, the Germans announced that the new volunteer corps was not part of *Nordland*, but would also be framed in the *Waffen SS*.

Danish volunteers in a recruitment center for the *Frikorps Danmark* and *Nordland* regiment.

Christian Peder Kryssing.

On that same day, the Danish government authorized its army officers to join the new voluntary formation, without suffering consequences. On 3 July, the Danish press and radio reported that the government had accepted the formation of this unit: "... *the Danish royal government has recognized the* Frikorps Danmark. *The* Frikorps *fights for the new Europe and for the cause of Denmark. The recruiting office of the* Frikorps Danmark *and the* Nordland *Regiment informs: Lieutenant Colonel Christian Peder Kryssing*[4], *commander of the Fifth Artillery Detachment 'Holbaek', has assumed command of the* Frikorps Danmark *with the approval of the Danish Royal Government, of the whose formation he had already been informed. The Chief of Staff of* Frikorps Danmark *is Captain Thor Jörgensen. The Corps will be under the command of Danish officers. Anyone who has served in the military since 1931 can enlist.* " Also on 3 July, a first group of 150 volunteers left for Hamburg.

On 8 July, the Danish government, through its Defense Minister, Sören Brorsen, sent a circular to all career soldiers, who were enlisting by the dozen in the new formation. In the circular the minister stated that: "*... the Danish government has authorized active duty career soldiers, reserve soldiers and Danish army recruits to enlist in* Frikorps Danmark. *of the reserve, after receiving the communication that they have been accepted, they must apply to leave their post temporarily, and then be reinstated at the end of their service in the Free Corps* ".

The first group of Danish volunteers before the departure for Germany, Summer 1941.

A Danish volunteer for the *Frikorps Danmark*, in a Recruitment center in Copenaghen, Summer 1941.

It was basically the official authorization of the government. Numerous career officers, including Kryssing himself, enlisted thanks to this document. After the war, Brorsen justified himself by saying that he had come under pressure from the German occupation authorities.

The name *Frikorps* (in German *Freikorps*), was chosen in memory of the Danish voluntary units that had fought during the wars of independence of Finland, Estonia and Latvia. After the collapse of the Tsarist Empire, Finland fought for its independence and during this struggle it counted on the support of a Swedish volunteer corps in which numerous Danish volunteers militated. They were later the nucleus of a Danish Free Corps which,

From the left, Kryssing and Thor Jörgensen.

under the command of Captain Richard Gustav Borgelin, fought for the liberation of Estonia and Latvia.

The recruiting campaign

Lieutenant Colonel Kryssing personally activated intense propaganda through the radio and the press, with the explicit support of members of the government and the leaders of the armed forces. Almost all of the unit's command posts were filled with Danish officers and NCOs. The motivations of these volunteers were very different from those of the first Danish volunteers for the *Nordland* regiment. In *Frikorps Danmark* they enlisted not for ideological affinity with National Socialism, but for a common cause, that of fighting communism. The use of the German uniform was a pure 'technical' necessity, Denmark being formally not at war with the USSR. In the first contingent of volunteers for *Frikorps*, barely a third of them were National Socialist activists or sympathizers. Recruitment centers were established throughout Denmark and volunteers came from all social classes.

Danish volunteers at Ryvangen camp, Summer 1941.

On July 7, Kryssing traveled to Berlin to confer with *SS-Gruf.* Gottlob Berger, head of the *SS-Hauptamt*. The Danish Lieutenant Colonel had set the following conditions for the formation of the unit:

1) the Frikorps would fight under the Danish flag

From the left, Per Sörensen and Thor Jörgensen.

2) all officers and soldiers had to be Danish and the language used would be Danish

3) the Frikorps would fight only against the Bosheviks and would remain a compact national unit within the German armed forces.

Kryssing also requested the use of Danish uniforms as well as national rank badges, however Berger explained to him the need for Danish volunteers to wear the same German uniform to avoid identification problems at the front, also because the Danish uniform was very similar. to the Soviet one. Eventually Kryssing and Berger came to a total understanding.

Meanwhile, in Denmark the recruitment campaign proceeded: on 15 July, the SS command established the official name of the Danish formation, as *'Freiwilligenverband Dänemark'*, transferring an officer and 108 Danish soldiers who had already enlisted in the SS *Nordwest* Regiment to it.

The commander Kryssing, on the right, with German officers at Ryvangen camp, July 1941.

Danish volunteers before the departure for Germany.

The train with the volunteers heading for Hamburg.

The Danish volunteers at the oath of allegiance.

During the departure ceremony of the second contingent of Danish volunteers, about 480 men, for Hamburg, celebrated on July 19 at the Ryvangen camp, Lieutenant Colonel Kryssing gave the following speech: "... *Thank you for joining the Korps and thanks also to the Danish government for recognizing* Freikorps .... *Thanks because we can raise our flag again and use the Danish language as command language* ". According to the plans of the German command, the *Freikorps* was to be organized as a motorized infantry regiment and for this reason, at least initially, with the first volunteers left for Germany, the first battalion of the same would be formed.

Transfer to Germany

After the ceremony at Ryvangen camp, Danish volunteers marched to the Hellerup railway station. After a brief stop at Copenhagen Central Station, the convoy left for Hamburg, where it arrived on July 20. The Danish volunteers were quartered in the Langenhorn camp, located in the northern part of the city. Here, the four Danish companies received the SS uniforms. On August 5, 1941, the first swearing-in ceremony to the flag took place, in Danish: the officers still wore the Danish uniform, while the troops were already wearing the SS uniform. The Danish volunteers were not required to take an oath of allegiance to Hitler, but on the advice of Kryssing, the following formula was found: "... *I soon in the name of God this oath, that in the fight against Bolshevism I unconditionally accept obedience to the Supreme Commander of the Wehrmacht, Adolf Hitler and like a good soldier I am ready to give my life for this oath. "*

The *Dannebrog* was brought forward at the oath of allegiance (NARA).

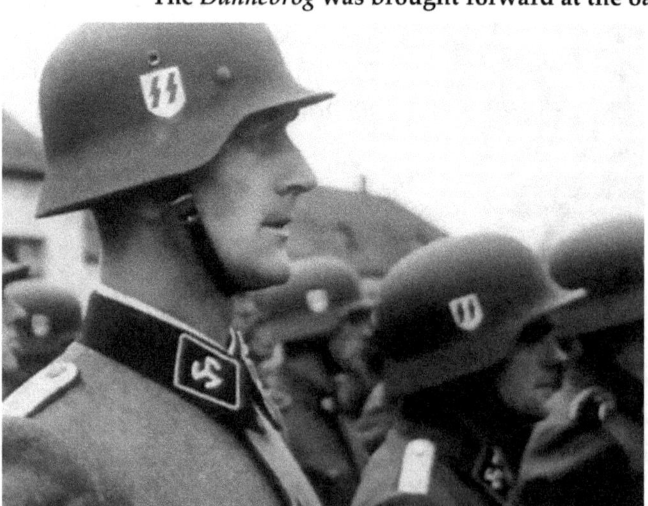

SS-Ostuf. **Per Sörensen with *Trifos* collar badge, 1941.**

As a collar badge, the volunteers adopted the three-armed solar wheel or *Trifos*: initially this insignia had been used precisely for the *Nordwest* Regiment. On July 12, the SS command decided to authorize it also for the Danish volunteers of the *Frikorps*, although many preferred to use the normal double runes.

Command structure

On August 10, 1941, another three hundred new Danish volunteers arrived. Later, some Danish officers and non-commissioned officers from *Wiking* were transferred to *Frikorps* to occupy command posts. Basic education continued, but fortunately sixty per cent of the volunteers were former soldiers of the Danish armed

SS-Ostubaf. **Christian Peder Kryssing.**

The weapons had to be cleaned, inspected and oiled.

forces and therefore already partially trained. In early September 1941, the command structure of the *Frikorps Danmark* was as follows:

<u>Commander</u>: *SS-Ostubaf.* C. Peder Kryssing
<u>Stabschef</u> (*Ia*): *SS-Stubaf.* Thor Jørgensen
<u>Adjutant</u>: *SS-Ustuf.* Kjærgaard Rasmussen
<u>Stabs-Kompanie</u> (company of the General Staff): 6 officers and 102 non-commissioned officers and soldiers
<u>1.Kompanie</u>: *SS-Hstuf.* Winding-Christensen (4 officers and 108 non-commissioned officers and soldiers)
<u>2.Kompanie</u>: *SS-Hstuf.* Knud Borg Martinsen (4 officers and 175 non-commissioned officers and soldiers)
<u>3.Kompanie</u>: *SS-Hstuf.* Olaf Krabbe (4 officers and 193 non-commissioned officers and soldiers)
<u>4. (schwere).Kompanie</u>: *SS-Hstuf.* S.Schock (3 officers and 200 non-commissioned officers and soldiers)
<u>Ersatz Kompanie</u> (reinforcement company): *SS-Hstuf.* Fr. Neergaard Jacobsen (12 officers)

<u>Total strength</u>: 38 officers, 858 non-commissioned officers and soldiers.

It should be noted that for the officers' ranks, we indicated the normal SS prefix, while in reality, for the Germanic volunteers enrolled in the voluntary formations of the *Waffen-SS*, such as the *Frikorps Danmark*, the prefix Legions was normally used (for example *Legions- Hauptsturmführer*). Of course, officers who already came from other SS units, the prefix SS was used. A small German General Staff was also added to the Danish formation to facilitate training operations.

Danish volunteers at Langenhorn camp (*Lars Larsen*).

Danish volunteers in training at Treskau camp, 1941.

The first three companies each received a German officer, while the fourth, two. Each rifle company was formed by three platoons, the fourth was initially formed by a platoon of light mortars, two of heavy mortars and one of machine guns. Subsequently it was restructured on three platoons of heavy machine guns and one of heavy mortars. During the training period, the three machine gun platoons were assigned to the three rifle companies. The formation of a new fourth heavy weapons company was then initiated, comprising two platoons of light infantry guns, one anti-tank platoon and one pioneer.

During the month of September, the backup company reached 296 and soon after these recruits were transferred to the Reinforcement Battalion of the German Legions in Graz, Austria, for further training.

Transfer to Treskau

On September 15, 1941, the *Frikorps Danmark* was transferred to the General Government of Poland, at the Posen-Treskau education camp, near Poznan, where it was fully equipped and motorized. The training proceeded rapidly: a German training General Staff, under the orders of the *SS-Hstuf.* Paul Massel[5], supervised the activities of the *Frikorps* to ensure the German rules of military education. Naturally all the officers and non-commissioned officers of the General Staff of education were subordinated to the SS High Command and not to *Frikorps*.

Training in accurate shooting at Treskau camp, 1941 (*Lars Larsen*).

SS-Hstuf. **Knud Børge Martinsen.**

Unfortunately, the German instructors were particularly severe with the Danish volunteers, which caused disagreements between Massel and Kryssing. The Danish commander himself, from the beginning of the training sessions, proved unsuitable for his role: coming from the artillery, he did not have very clear ideas about how an infantry unit should be commanded on the field. Even *SS-Stubaf.* Thor Jørgensen himself, did not prove to be up to the role assigned to him and was dismissed. At the beginning of November, 'ideological' conflicts between Kryssing and the German military authorities also began to emerge: the Danish commander wanted to form an apolitical military national unit, while the Germans wanted to exploit the Legion's high propaganda value. Between December and February 1942, Kryssing was called several times to Berlin, to resolve the issue, but in the end the Danish officer and his son Jens, also enlisted in the *Frikorps*, resigned. Kryssing was transferred as an artillery officer to the *Totenkopf* General Staff and *SS-Hstuf.* Knud Børge Martinsen[6] was temporarily placed in command of the *Frikorps Danmark*.

SS-Rottenführer **Elton Jensen,** *Kriegsberichter* **in the** *'Kurt Eggers'* **unit with the Danish arm shield.**

Danish volunteers with the first version Flag.

Flags, arm shields and cuff bands

As for other European national legions, also for the Danish legion, on November 17, 1941, an arm shield with the colors of the Danish flag, red with a white cross, was authorized to be worn on the left arm of the uniform. Initially some of these shields were made by the volunteers themselves, using strips of white cloth for the cross on a red shield, then later they were printed in various shapes. A cuff band with the inscription *'Freikorps Danmark'* was also authorized at the same time: the inscription *Freikorps* was in German (*Frikorps* in Danish) and *Danmark* in Danish (*Dänemark* in German). A first model of the band, used Gothic characters, with only the writing in silver on a black background, the second model was made with Latin characters, on the model of the other cuff bands of the SS units. For the Danish legion, an official flag was also authorized, practically the same as the Danish flag with the addition of *'Frikorps Danmark'*. Later a second version was adopted, square in shape, with a white Teutonic-style cross, again on a red background.

New commander

Among the many problems that arose around the formation of the Danish unit, there was also that of its employment at the front. The SS High Command thought about how to use this small unit, with the strength of a battalion and the fairest thing seemed to be to integrate it into a larger German unit. On March 21, 1942, Himmler wrote to Fritz Clausen, the Danish National Socialist leader, to propose that he integrate the Danish

in World War Two 1939-1945

The second version of Danish flag.

SS-Stubaf. von Schalburg. Note the Danish arm shield on your uniform.

volunteers into a new German-Danish SS Regiment, which was to be called *'Thule'*. However, this initiative was not successful and even if the Regiment was actually created and subsequently assigned to the SS *Totenkopf* division, it never counted Danish volunteers among its ranks.

For their part, the Danes wanted to preserve the national character of their unit and such was their insistence that in April 1942, the Command of the *Waffen-SS*, authorized a special insignia for the *Frikorps*: a small Danish flag instead of the double runes or the *Trifos*. Practically this insignia was used only during the period of training and within the company.

In March 1942, *SS-Stubaf.* von Schalburg took over the command of *Frikorps Danmark*, a veteran of the battles with the *Wiking* and decorated with both classes of the Iron Cross: during the first months of the campaign in the East, he found himself several times under enemy fire at the command of fighting groups. He was in charge of dangerous reconnaissance missions and thanks to his perfect knowledge of the Russian language, he crossed enemy lines several times. *SS-Gruf.* Steiner himself, claimed that he was one of the most capable, intelligent and valiant men in *Wiking*. However, the appointment of von Schalburg had a purely political significance for the SS High Command: as soon as von Schalburg arrived in command of the *Frikorps*, the German training liaison group was dissolved and the *SS-Stubaf.* Massel returned to the *SS-Hauptamt* in Berlin. Von Schalburg immediately began a rigorous training program for combat readiness, completed with the use of heavy weapons and defensive improvisation techniques. The arrival of von Schalburg raised the spirits of the volunteers eager to be transferred to the front as soon as possible, knowing that the new commander was an experienced and decorated veteran. In any case, to avoid misunderstandings, with the volunteers who were not National Socialists, *SS-Stubaf.* von

C.F. von Schalburg, the *Freikorps* commander, takes part in a field exercise (*Lars Larsen*).

Danish volunteers in training at the Treskau camp.

Schalburg himself, during the presentation ceremony, made it clear: "*... I hope that none of you will join the Party. because of me. But from those who are already members of the same, I will demand double, because you have two reasons for which to fight: for the Party and for the fight against Bolshevism* ".

Departure for the front

At the end of April 1942, the order came from the *SS-Hauptamt* for the *Frikorps* to be transferred to the front line, along with the latest equipment and means of transport for the unit. In early May, von Schalburg was called to Berlin to be briefed on details about the use of the *Frikorps*. During the night between 6 and 7 May, all departments were put on alert. Testimony of the *SS-Hstuf*. Martinsen: "*.... When the alarm was raised everyone thought it was just a test. Only when the motorized columns set off for Posen did we begin to understand that it was getting serious ...*". Upon leaving for the front, the *Frikorps* battle order was as follows:

Soldiers of *Frikorps Danmark* during training.

Commander: *SS-Stubaf.* von Schalburg
Adjutant: *SS-Ustuf.* Eduard Hein[7]
Information Officer: *SS-Ostuf.* Gerd von Reitzenstein[8]
Ordinance Officer: *SS-Ustuf.* Thorgils
Intendency officers: *SS-Hstuf.* Bayer, *SS-Ustuf.* Salskov and *SS-Ustuf.* Petersen
Transportation officers: *SS-Ustuf.* Wolf and *SS-Hscha.* Krog
Medical officer: *SS-Ustuf.* Dr. Lotze

1.*Kompanie*
Commander: *SS-Ostuf.* Per Sörensen
Zugführer: *SS-Ustuf.* Just Nielsen, *SS-Ustuf.* Karl Wahle, *SS-Oscha.* Leo Madsen, *SS-Oscha.* Stadtscheid

2.*Kompanie*
Commander: *SS-Ostuf.* Boy-Hansen
Zugführer: *SS-Ostuf.* Worsøe-Larsen, *SS-Ustuf.* Poulsen, *SS-Ustuf.* Jensen, *SS-Ustuf.* Dombeck, *SS-Ustuf.* von Eggers, *SS-Hscha.* H.P. Jensen

3.*Kompanie*
Commander: *SS-Hstuf.* Per Neergaard-Jacobsen
Zugführer: *SS-Ostuf.* Henneke, *SS-Ustuf.* Fenger, *SS-Ustuf.* Nordholm, *SS-Ustuf.* Alfred Nielsen

4.*Kompanie*
Commander: *SS-Hstuf.* K.B. Martinsen
Zugführer: *SS-Ostuf.* Stenger, *SS-Ustuf.* Kure, *SS-Ustuf.* Dürkopf, *SS-Oscha.* Klinger

Notes

[1] Christian Frederik von Schalburg was born on April 15, 1906 in Zmeinogorsk, imperial Russia, the first of three children of August Theodor Schalburg and his wife Helene Schalburg. His father was born in 1870 in Nyborg in Denmark, while his mother Elena Vasiljevna born Starizki von Siemianowska, was born in 1882 in Ukraine, from a noble Russian family. As a young man, Schalburg received a military education in the cadet corps of the Tsar and lived in Russia until the October Revolution of 1917, when his family fled to Denmark. This dramatic event marked his life and gave rise to his hatred of communism. In 1925, he enlisted in the King's personal guard. In 1929, he married Baroness

Christian Frederik von Schalburg.

Helga Frederikke von Bülow. Although politically a conservative, after Hitler's rise to power in Germany, he began to approach National Socialism and was one of the first Danish officers to join the DNSAP, the National Socialist Party of the Danish Workers. On November 22, 1934, Alexander's son was born. In 1937, he was promoted to captain of the King's Personal Guard. From January 1939, he was placed in charge of the youth section (NSU, *National-Socialistiske Ungdom*, National Socialist youth) of the DNSAP, where he became very popular. At the end of the same year, together with many young Danes, he volunteered to Finland to fight against the Soviets. When the Germans invaded Denmark on April 9, 1940, Schalburg was still abroad and despite his National Socialist faith he was very upset that his country had surrendered without a fight. In September 1940, with the consent of the Danish army and the King, von Schalburg was one of the first officers to enlist in the *Waffen-SS*, serving in the II./Germany of the *Wiking* and then as first ordinance officer of the chief of staff of the division with the rank of *SS-Hauptsturmführer*. Despite this 'administrative' role, he was often engaged in the field, also leading dangerous missions on the Eastern front, pushing himself into enemy territory, thanks to his perfect knowledge of the Russian language. These actions earned him the granting of both classes of the Iron Cross and promotion to the rank of *SS-Sturmbannführer*.

[2] Rudolf Jensen, born on 30 April 1899 in Flensburg, SS-Nr. 48 230. He will later serve in the *SS-Hauptamt*.

[3] The Anti-Comintern Pact was signed on November 25, 1936 in Berlin, as a pact of political alliance between the government of the German Third Reich and the Japanese Empire, for a "*... common defense against the disintegrating work of the international Communist*". On November 6, 1937, Italy also joined. In February 1939 Hungary and Manchukuo also joined the Pact and on April 15, 1939 it was Spain's turn. In November 1941, the accession of the satellite states of Germany, namely Romania, Bulgaria, Croatia, and Slovakia, and of the Chinese government of Wang Jingwei was registered.

[4] Christian Peder Kryssing, born on 7 July 1891 in Kolding, an artillery officer in the Danish army and a fervent anti-communist.

[5] Paul Massel, born on 30 May 1909 in Stolp in Pomerania, SS-Nr. 261 914. Previously he had served in the *III./Sta. 'Deutschland'*, in command of the *7./Sta. 'Der Führer'*. Later he will pass to the command of *Begl.Btl. RFSS*.

[6] Knud Børge Martinsen, born November 30, 1905 in Sandved, a Danish army officer and member of the DNSAP.

[7] Eduard Hein, born October 2, 1909 in Wernstad, SS-Nr. 332 287. Later commanded the *14./Danmark* and would fall on January 22, 1944 on the Leningrad front.

[8] Gerd von Reitzenstein, born on 20 August 1918 in Berlin, SS-Nr. 311 267. he would later command the *7./Danmark* before being transferred to *12.SS-Pz.Div. 'Hitlerjugend'* in command of the *5./SS-Pz.Aufkl.Abt.12*.

Bibliografia

Massimiliano Afiero,"*Frikorps Danmark: i volontari danesi sul fronte dell'Est, 1941-1943*", Associazione Culturale Ritterkreuz

Jens Pank Bjerregaard, Lars Larsen, "*Danish Volunteers of the Waffen-SS: Freikorps Danmark 1941-43*", Helion & Co Ltd

Richard Landwehr, "*La Estirpe de Thor: el cuerpo franco SS Danés en la campana de Rusia, 1941-43*", Garcia Hispan Editor

Richard Landwehr, & Holger Thor Nielsen, "*Nordic Warriors – SS-Panzergrenadier-Regiment 24 Danmark, Eastfront, 1943-45*", Shelf Books Ldt., 1999.

General der Waffen-SS
Georg Keppler: a biographical chronology
by Michael D. Miller
with translation assistance from Gary Costello

SS-Obergruppenführer und General der Waffen-SS **Georg Keppler in 1944.**

in World War Two 1939-1945

Major Keppler in *Heer* uniform, 1935. (*SS-Personalakte Keppler*).

SS-Stubaf. **Keppler with Rudolf Hess and Heinrich Himmler in 1936.** (*Max Williams*)

Georg Heinrich Keppler
SS-Obergruppenführer und General der Waffen-SS

*: 07.05.1894 in Mainz/Hessen.

†: 16.06.1966 in Hamburg.

NSDAP-Nr.: 338.211 (Joined 01.10.1930)
SS-Nr.: 273.799 (Joined 10.10.1935)

Promotions

28.02.1913: *Fahnenjunker*
00.00.1914: *Fähnrich*
18.06.1914: *Leutnant (mit Patent vom 23.06.1912)*
18.10.1917: *Oberleutnant*
21.06.1920: *Polizeihauptmann*
01.07.1931: *Polizeimajor*
24.05.1935: *Major*
10.10.1935: *SS-Sturmbannführer*
20.04.1937: *SS-Obersturmbannführer*
20.04.1938: *SS-Standartenführer*
13.05.1940: *SS-Oberführer*
09.11.1940: *SS-Brigadeführer und Generalmajor der Waffen-SS*
30.01.1942: *SS-Gruppenführer und Generalleutnant der Waffen-SS*
25.05.1944: *SS-Obergruppenführer und General der Waffen-SS (mit Wirkung vom 21.06.1944)*

Career

ca. 1900-ca. 1904: *Volksschule.*

ca. 1904-00.02.1913: *Alten Gymnasium* in Bremen (passed his Abitur, 00.02.1913).

28.02.1913-00.00.1915(?): Entered service as *Fahnenjunker*, assigned to *Füsilier-Regiment "Generalfeldmarschall Prinz Albrecht von Preussen" (Hannoversches) Nr. 73* (Hannover).

Attended *Kriegsschule* in Glogau/Schlesien, 00.10.1913-00.05.1914, then returned to his regiment. He was then assigned successively as a *Zugführer*, *Kompanieführer*, and *Regiments-Adjutant* from 00.00.1914 to 29.08.1914.

29.08.1914-00.00.1915 (?): Severely wounded near St. Quentin, then hospitalized.

SS-Staf. **Keppler speaks with Peter Hansen during training exercises in 1939.**

Formal portrait of *SS-Obf.* Keppler after he was decorated with the *Ritterkreuz*, 1940.

00.00.1915-11.11.1918: Assigned successively as *Brigade-Ordonnanz-Offizier* of *39. Infanterie-Brigade*; *Divisions-Ordonnanz-Offizier* of *19. Reserve-Division*; and *Regiments-Adjutant* of *Füsilier-Regiment 73*. He sustained a further two wounds by war's end.

00.11.1918-00.08.1919: Assigned to *Infanterie-Regiment "von Courbiere" Nr. 19* (Posen), later redesignated *Reichswehr-Infanterie-Regiment 19*.

04.08.1919-01.10.1924: Joined the *Sicherheitswehr Hannover* (redesignated as the *Schutzpolizei Hannover*, 01.02.1920), assigned as *Gruppen-Adjutant*.

09.10.1924-30.06.1926: *Führer* of a *Hundertschaft* of the *Schutzpolizei Hannover*.

01.07.1926: Discharged from the *Preussischen Polizei "aus politischen und persönlichen Gründen..."* (on political and personal grounds) and transferred to the *Landespolizei* in Thüringen.

01.07.1926-31.12.1926: Assigned to the *Polizeiabteilung* in Gotha.

01.01.1927-14.02.1928: *Führer* of the *selbständigen Hundertschaft* in Hildburghausen.

15.02.1928-30.06.1930: *Referent für Polizeiangelegenheiten, Organisation, Einsatz usw.* (Advisor for Police Affairs, Organization, Operations, etc.) to the *Chef der Landespolizei Thüringen*.

01.07.1930-14.11.1933: *Kommandeur der Schutzpolizei* in Jena.

01.10.1930: Joined the NSDAP.

15.11.1933-24.05.1935: *Kommandeur der Landespolizei-Abteilung* in Gotha.

24.05.1935: Submitted his application for admission to the *politischen Bereitschaften der SS* (political readiness detachments of the SS, soon redesignated *SS-Verfügungstruppe*), as

Formal portraits of *SS-Oberführer* Keppler taken shortly after he was decorated with the *Ritterkreuz*, 1940.

follows:

It is my greatest wish to put all of my available energy into the National Socialist movement. With the absorption of the Landespolizei into the Reichswehr, the possibility of doing this is substantially limited. I therefore ask whether my transfer to the political readiness detachments of the SS is possible. (SS-Personalakte Keppler)

24.05.1935-10.10.1935: Transferred from the *Landespolizei* to the *Heer* with the rank of *Major*, assigned to *Infanterie-Regiment 32/ 24. Infanterie-Division* (Teplitz-Schönau). Discharged at his own request.

10.10.1935-23.03.1938: Joined the SS, assigned as *Führer* of *I. Sturmbann/SS-Standarte 1/SS-Verfügungstruppe* (München).

[00.00.1937]: *Schiedhelfer für den kleinen Schiedhof beim Reichsführer-SS* (arbitrator's assistant for the small arbitration court attached to the *Reichsführer-SS*), München.

23.03.1938-11.07.1941: *Führer* of *SS-Standarte 3 der SS-Verfügungstruppe* (Wien) ("beauftragt mit der Aufstellung und Führung" [charged with formation and leadership] until 20.04.1938, then permanent). Redesigned *SS-Standarte "Der Führer"*, 17.08.1938, and *SS-Regiment (mot.) "Der Führer"* on 01.12.1940. He led this regiment in the annexation of the Sudetenland (with his headquarters in Znaim), 01.10.1938-00.10.1938 and in the Western Campaign of May/June 1940.

00.06.1939-00.09.1939: *Kommandeur* of *SS-Wachbataillon Prag*, the personal guard unit of the *Reichsprotektor Böhmen und Mähren*, Constantin Freiherr von Neurath.

30.09.1940: In an evaluation report of that date, the divisional commander of the *SS-V-Division*, *SS-Gruppenführer* Paul Hausser, described Keppler as follows:

Thoroughly decent, forthright character, especially trustworthy.

04.09.1940: Georg Keppler as *Kommandeur* of *SS-Regiment "Der Führer"* and Divisional Commander Paul Hausser during the *Ritterkreuz* ceremony for *SS-Untersturmführer* Ludwig Kepplinger. (*NARA, photos by SS-Kriegsberichter Paul Augustin*).

Georg Keppler and *SS-Ustuf.* Ludwig Kepplinger.

Clear headed, strong-willed. Outstanding soldier, As regiment commander proven through prudent and strong leadership; it was recognized by the award of the Ritterkreuz. An ideologically stable National Socialist, fills position fully. Suitable for Div. Kdr.

Div. Stu. Qu. 30.09.40

[Signed] Hausser
SS-Gruppenführer
Kommandeur SS-V.Division

(*SS-Personalakte Keppler*)

07.02.1941-11.02.1941: Attended a *"Lehrgang für Divisions-Kommandeure"* (Instructional course for divisional commanders) in Jena.

00.03.1941-00.03.1941: In Italy for a 14-day lecture tour.

15.07.1941-21.09.1941: *"Vertretungsweise beauftragt mit der Führung der SS-Division 'Totenkopf'"* on the northern sector of the Eastern Front.

09.09.1941: Briefly charged with leadership of *SS-Kampfgruppe "Nord"* as successor to

SS-Brigadeführer Keppler on the Eastern Front, Summer 1941.

An autographed portrait of *SS-Brigdf.* **Keppler, 1941.** (*Roger Bender*)

Karl-Maria Demelhuber, but due to acute illness, he was unable to assume this function.

21.09.1941-01.04.1942: Under a physician's care due to meningitis.

07.02.1942-11.02.1942: Again attended the *"Lehrgang für Divisions-Kommandeure"* in Jena.

01.04.1942-10.02.1943: *Kommandeur* of *SS-Division "Das Reich"* (redesignated *SS-Panzer-Grenadier-Division "Das Reich"*, 09.11.1942). Forced to relinquish command due to illness (meningitis).

10.02.1943-30.08.1943: Again under a doctor's care due to meningitis.

31.08.1943-20.03.1944: *Befehlshaber der Waffen-SS Böhmen-Mähren.* (Prag).

20.03.1944-06.04.1944: Placed in *Führerreserve der Waffen-SS im SS-Führungshauptamt*, with simultaneous attachment to the *Kommandostab RFSS*. During this period, assigned by the *Reichsführer-SS* as *Sonderbevollmächtigter zur Erfassung von Personal für die Front* (Special Plenipotentiary for Requisitioning of Personnel for the Front).

06.04.1944-31.10.1944: *Befehlshaber der Waffen-SS Ungarn* (Budapest).

11.08.1944 - 24.10.1944: *"Vertretungsweise beauftragt mit der Führung"* (charged with acting leadership) of *II. SS-Panzer-Korps* on the Western Front, assuming temporary command from Wilhelm Bittrich who was supposedly *"erkrankten"* (ill) but had in fact been temporarily relieved of command due to insubordination against the *Reichsführer-SS*. Bittrich retained overall command due to the protection of *General der Panzertruppe* Heinrich Eberbach and *Generalfeldmarschall* Walter Model.

16.08.1944-24.10.1944: *Kommandierender General* of *I. SS-Panzer-Korps "Leibstandarte"* (acting until 31.08.1944, then permanent) on the Western Front. Succeeded Josef "Sepp" Dietrich, who had moved to command of *5. Panzer-Armee* on 09.08.1944 (Dietrich's chief of staff, Fritz Kraemer, held interim command from that date until the arrival of Keppler a week later). Keppler was succeeded by Hermann Priess. Keppler's postwar manuscript *"I SS Panzer Corps (16 Aug.-18 Oct 1944)"*, written for the U.S. Army Historical Division in 1946, provides detailed information on formations actions during the period of his command.

Summer 1941: Keppler (left) as acting *Kommandeur* of the *SS-Totenkopf-Division* in conversation with Karl Wolff and Matthias Kleinheisterkamp. (*NARA, SS-Kriegsberichter Ernst Baumann*)

SS-Gruf. **Georg Keppler. (*Roger Bender*)**

29.10.1944-04.02.1945: Transferred to the *SS-Führungshauptamt/Führerreserve der Waffen-SS* with simultaneous attachment- effective 30.10.1944- to *III. (Germanische) SS-Panzer-Korps* as *Vertreter* (deputy, in effect acting commander) to the Kom. Gen., Felix Steiner (who was ill). Succeeded by Matthias Kleinheisterkamp.

01.11.1944-05.02.1945: *Befehlshaber der Waffen-SS beim Höheren SS- und Polizeiführer Ungarn* (Commander of the Waffen-SS attached to the Higher SS and Police Leader in Hungary [Dr. Otto Winkelmann]). He never actually assumed the duties of this post, as Karl Pfeffer-Wildenbruch, since 01.09.1944 assigned as acting *Befehlshaber der Waffen-SS in Ungarn*, remained in the post.

12.02.1945-26.04.1945: *Kommandierender General* of *XVIII. SS-Armee-Korps*, a component of Paul

Hausser's *Heeresgruppe G*, on the Western Front (Alsace and the Schwarzwald [Black Forest]). Succeeded Heinz Reinefarth. This formation was encircled in the Schwarzwald on 22.04.1945 and dissolved on 26.04.1945.

SS-Brif.u.Gen.Maj.d.W-SS Keppler at *Führer* Headquarters, Autumn 1941. Top photo, left to right: Alfred Jodl, Dr.-Ing. Fritz Todt, and Keppler. Bottom photo: Hitler, Jodl, and Keppler.

Published Work

"*B-155, I SS Panzer Corps (16 Aug.-18 Oct 1944)*" (in "Manuscripts assembled under the Foreign Military Studies Program of the Historical Division, U.S. Army Europe, 1945-54;

SS-Gruf.u.Gen.Lt.d.W-SS **Georg Keppler.** (*Max Williams*)

SS-Ogruf.u.Gen.d.W-SS **Keppler in 1944.**

written in 1946, published in 1954).

Postwar Confinement and Activities

22.05.1945-26.04.1948: Captured by U.S. Army troops in the vicinity of Seebrück, then delivered to the U.S. 7th Army Interrogation Center, Augsburg the following day. He was subsequently held at internment camps in Seckenheim, Kornwestheim, Hersfeld, Allendorf, Neustadt, and in hospital in Garmisch.

00.04.1948-00.12.1952: Worked from his home and as a *Gemeindeschreiber* (communal recorder) in Oberbayern.

01.01.1953-00.05.1961: Commercial employee, and from 1954 onward *Prokurist* (company secretary) of a chemical company in Hamburg.

00.05.1961: Retired.

Decorations & Awards

14.08.1940: *Ritterkreuz des Eisernen Kreuzes* as *SS-Oberführer* and *Kommandeur* of *SS-Regiment "Der Führer"/SS-Verfügungs-Division/18. Armee/Heeresgruppe B*, Western Campaign. Award based on *"Vorschlagsliste Nr. 2 für die Verleihung des Ritterkreuzes des Eisernen Kreuzes"* dated 01.07.1940 and signed by Div.-Kdr. Paul Hausser:

The SS V Division proposes the award of the Ritterkreuz des Eisernen Kreuzes to SS Oberführer Keppler, Kommandeur SS "Der Führer".

Justification: The Regt. SS "Der Führer" was the only infantry regiment within the K.A.K. to force a breakthrough through the Grebbe Line. The rapidity has had far-reaching operational consequences. The surrender of Fortress Holland and the Dutch Army were brought about by this. In reconnaissance, deployment, and command of his regiment. Oberführer Keppler distinguished himself through bravery in his personal commitment. He personally led the III. Btl. on the daring crossing of the Issl and the assault of the Grebbe Mountain under heavy enemy machine gun and artillery fire. Convinced that the breakthrough

through this key position would be a decisive action for further movement, SS-Oberführer Keppler, through his personal commitment, endured this fierce battle with his regiment, which naturally cost heavy casualties. It was only later that it became clear that the valiant efforts of the commander and his regiment had had such far-reaching consequences for the defense of the Fortress Holland.

Three photos of *SS-Gruf.* Keppler as Kdr. of *SS-Pz.Gren.Div. "Das Reich"* inspecting the division's supply elements, ca. Summer 1942. (*Dieter Ruetten*)

Keppler inspecting the division's supply elements.

Remarks: On 17.6.40, the SS-V.-Division made a request to the von Kleist Gruppe, through A.O.K. 18 and Gen. Kdo. K.A.K. to check whether the Ritterkreuz could not be awarded for the action of SS-Oberführer Keppler for the assault of the Grebbe Line. Copy of this Div. application can no longer be provided, as it was destroyed by fire when a command vehicle was lost in action against enemy combat vehicles that had broken through on 24.6.40. Report by the Kdr. SS "Der Führer" is included.

Div. St.Qu., 1 July 1940
[Signed] Hausser.
(SS-Personalakte Keppler; Translation courtesy of Gary Costello)

13.05.1940: *1939 Spange zum 1914 Eisernes Kreuz I. Klasse*

13.05.1940: *1939 Spange zum 1914 Eisernes Kreuz II. Klasse*

00.00.191_: *1914 Eisernes Kreuz I. Klasse*

00.00.191_: *1914 Eisernes Kreuz II. Klasse*

00.00.191_: *Hamburgisches Hanseatenkreuz*

00.00.191_: *Braunschweiger Kriegsverdienstkreuz II. Klasse am Band für Kämpfer*

00.00.19__: *Schlesischer Adler 1. Stufe*

00.00.19__: *Schlesischer Adler 2. Stufe*

ca. 1918: *Verwundetenabzeichen, 1918 in Silber*

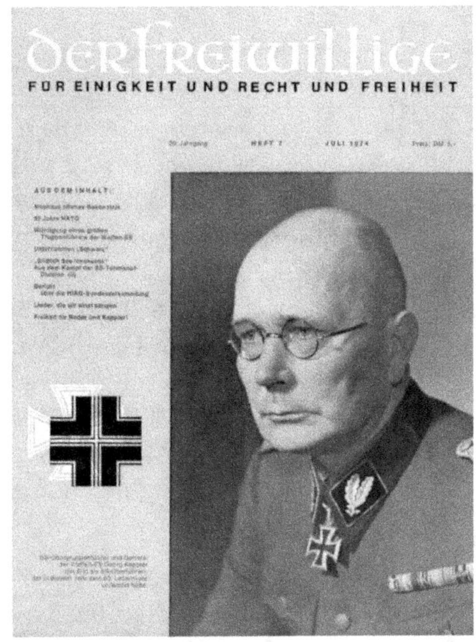

Der Freiwillige **honors the late Georg Keppler on the occasion of his 80th birthday.** (*Author's collection*)

ca. 1939: *Spange "Prager Burg" zur Medaille zur Erinnerung an den 1. Oktober 1938*
ca. 1939: *Medaille zur Erinnerung an den 1. Oktober 1938*
ca. 1939: *Medaille zur Erinnerung an den 13. März 1938*
ca. 1934: *Ehrenkreuz des Weltkrieges 1914-1918 mit Schwertern*
00.00.193_: *Deutsches Reiterabzeichen in Silber*
[01.12.1936]: *Ehrendegen des Reichsführers-SS*
[01.03.1938]: *Totenkopfring der SS*
00.00.193_: *SS-Zivilabzeichen* (Nr. 133.519)
16.12.1935: *Julleuchter der SS*

Notes

* Son of *Oberst a. D.* Johannes *Otto* Keppler (*27.10.1854, †16.11.1936) and his wife Amalie Elisabeth Keppler, née Heyke (*21.05.1870). He had one sister, Louise Ida *Elisabeth* Gaertig (*20.06.1892 in Mainz, †18.05.1953 in Blankenburg/Harz).
* Religion: Protestant. Left the church and declared himself *gottgläubig*, 00.00.19__.
* Married on 01.02.1922 to Elisabeth Crudup (*07.12.1897 in Krotoschin/Provinz Posen; NSDAP-Nr. 338.212, daughter of *Generalmajor* Karl Hermann Crudup (*29.06.1845 in Verden/Hannover). Two children resulted from this marriage:
  - Horst Keppler (*25.01.1922 in Hannover, †13.05.1940 at Donchery near Sedan). Killed in action as a *Schütze* in *3. Kompanie/Schützen-Regiment 2*.
  - Elisabeth Keppler (*13.09.1923).
* Foreign language proficiency: French.

Sources

Miller, Michael D. & Schulz, Andreas: *Leaders of the SS & German Police, Volume 2 (Reichsführer-SS – SS-Gruppenführer/Hans Haltermann to Walter Krüger)*. R. James Bender Publishing, 2015.
National Archives and Records Administration, College Park, Maryland: *SS-Personalakte of Georg Keppler*. Microfilm document collection A3343SS. - *Interrogation Records Prepared for War Crimes Proceedings at Nuernberg, 1945-1947/OCCPAC Interrogation Transcripts and Related Records: - Keppler, Georg Heinrich*; Publication Number M1270, Record Group RG238.
Nix, Philip: *Biographical Notes from the archives of Mr. Nix, Birmingham, England*.
Schulz, Andreas & Zinke, Dr. Dieter: *Die Generale der Waffen-SS und der Polizei 1933-1945, Band 2 (Hachtel-Kutschera)*. Biblio-Verlag, 2005.
Yerger, Mark C.: *Waffen-SS Commanders: Augsberger to Kreutz*. Schiffer Military History, 1997.
SS-Personalkanzlei and SS-Personalhauptamt: *Dienstaltersliste der Schutzstaffel der NSDAP, Stand vom 1. Dezember 1936*.
    - *Dienstaltersliste der Schutzstaffel der NSDAP, Stand vom 1. Dezember 1937*.
    - *Dienstaltersliste der Schutzstaffel der NSDAP, Stand vom 1. Dezember 1938*.
    - *Dienstaltersliste der Schutzstaffel der NSDAP, Stand vom 30. Januar 1942*.
    - *Dienstaltersliste der Schutzstaffel der NSDAP, Stand vom 20. April 1942*.
    - *Dienstaltersliste der Schutzstaffel der NSDAP, Stand vom 9. November 1944*.

Italian Holders of the Iron Cross
by Hugh Page Taylor

Capitano di Fregata Conte Carlo Fecia Cossato.

The statutes of the Iron Cross, first established on 1 March 1813, and subsequently renewed for the Franco-Prussian War of 1870/1871 and the First World (or Great) War of 1914/1918, were renewed once again for WW2 on the day Germany started that conflict by invading Poland on 1 September 1939.

So much has been written about what is surely the best known, if not most prestigious German award, especially the holders of the various classes of the Knight's Cross, that one may be excused for asking *"what more can be said about it?"*. Unashamedly, this author continues to focus on Italian military matters by answering with another question: *"how many Italians were awarded the Iron Cross in WW2?"*

First let's consider the classes of the Knight's Cross and all of its non-German recipients.

The three highest classes, (i) Grand Cross, (ii) Golden Oak Leaves, Swords and Diamonds, and (iii) Oak Leaves Swords and Diamonds, were not awarded to any non-German, with *Generalfeldmarschall, Reichsminister der Luftfahrt und Oberbefehlshaber der Luftwaffe* Hermann Göring and *Luftwaffe Stuka* ace *Oberst* Hans-Ulrich Rudel being the sole recipients of the Grand Cross and the Golden Oak Leaves, Swords and Diamonds respectively on 19 July 1940 and 29 December 1944.

25 members of the *Wehrmacht* and 2 of the *Waffen-SS* received the Oak Leaves, Swords and Diamonds. No non-Germans received this award. Of the total of 160, just one non-German, Japanese Fleet Admiral Isoroku Yamamoto, so-called mastermind of the attack

in World War Two 1939-1945

Fleet Admiral Isoroku Yamamoto.

Generale di Corpo d'Armata Ugo Cavallero.

on Pearl Harbor, was awarded the Oak Leaves and Swords, posthumously on 27 May 1943, following his death at Kahili in East Asia on 18 April of that year.

Eight non-Germans received the Oakleaves, three Rumanians, two Japanese, one Spaniard, one Finn and one Belgian – but no Italians.

Italy came third in the ranking of non-German recipients of the Knight's Cross with nine, one of which being questionable as although it was awarded with great ceremony and publicity, it was withdrawn under not entirely clear circumstances after the war (see below under Enzo Grossi). Another Italian recipient is also reported, but no reference to him is to be found in published German sources, and no evidence has been forthcoming that he was indeed awarded the Knight's Cross[1].

Seventeen Rumanians and eight Hungarians were awarded the Knight's Cross, along with two Finns, two Spaniards, one Japanese and one Slovak.

Cavallero, Ugo

- Born: Casale Monferrato (Alessandria Province), 20 September 1880
- Rank at time of award: Lieutenant General (Generale di Corpo d'Armata)
- Command at time of award: Chief of the General Staff of the Italian Supreme Command
- RK awarded: 14 February 1942: motivation unconfirmed and questionable as he was of questionable military and leadership ability
- Found dead with handgun in hand in the garden of the Belvedere Hotel near Frascati on the morning of 14 September 1943, after having dined the previous evening with GFM Albert Kesselring (*Oberbefehlshaber Süd-West und Heeresgruppe C*) who later claimed he had appointed him to command a new fascist army: an appointment *SS-Standartenführer* Eugen Dollmann considered unlikely as Cavallero was *"completely compromised"* insofar as the Germans were concerned. Whether he committed suicide, was forced to do so, or was murdered remains a mystery.

Generale Ugo De Carolis.

Generale Fedele De Giorgis.

Generale Italo Gariboldi.

De Carolis, Ugo

- <u>Born</u>: Capua (Caserta Province), 7 October 1887
- <u>Rank at time of award</u>: Brigadier General (Generale di Brigata)
- <u>Command at time of award</u>: Infantry commander of the 52nd Infantry Division *"Torino"*, part of the Italian Expeditionary Corps (C.S.I.R.) in Russia
- <u>RK awarded</u>: posthumously 9 February 1942
- K.I.A. 12 December 1941 at Chazepetowka, Ukraine, Russian Front

De Giorgis[2], Fedele[3]

- <u>Born</u>: Chivasso (Turin Province), 17 January 1887
- <u>Rank at time of award</u>: Major General (Generale di Divisione)
- <u>Command at time of award</u>: C.O. 55th Infantry Division *"Savona"* in North Africa
- <u>RK awarded</u>: 9 January 1942, in which year he was forced to surrender to the British at Halfaya in Syria
- <u>Died</u>: 4 February 1964 in Rome

Fecia di Cossato, Conte Carlo

- <u>Born</u>: Rome, 25 September 1908
- <u>Rank at time of award</u>: Lieutenant Colonel (Capitano di Fregata)
- <u>Command at time of award</u>: Captain of submarine *"Enrico Tazzoli"*
- <u>RK awarded</u>: 19 March 1943 (EK2 on 30 June 1941 and EK1 in December 1941): between 15 April 1941 and 25 December 1942 as captain of the *"Enrico Tazzoli"* he had sunk 17 vessels totaling 88,317 GRT, with the sinking of what was believed to have been a British cruiser on 12 April 1941 unconfirmed
- Committed suicide in Naples on 27 August 1944

Gariboldi, Italo

- <u>Born</u>: Lodi , 20 April 1879
- <u>Rank at time of award</u>: Lieutenant General (Generale di Corpo d'Armata)
- <u>Command at time of award</u>: G.O.C. Italian 8th Army (8ª Armata Italiana, or ARMIR = Armata Italiana in Russia = Italian Army in Russia)
- <u>RK awarded</u>: 1 April 1943
- Died of natural causes in Rome, 9 February 1970

Generale di Corpo d'Armata Italo Gariboldi receiving his Knight's Cross from Hitler.

Capitano di Corvetta Gianfranco Gazzana-Priaroggia.

Gazzana-Priaroggia, Gianfranco

- <u>Born</u>: Milan, 30 August 1912
- <u>Rank at time of award</u>: Major (Capitano di Corvetta)
- <u>Command at time of award</u>: According to German RK records, captain of the submarine *"Archimede"*. Yet his most noted achievements were when he was captain of submarines *"Tazzoli"* and *"Leonardo da Vinci"*, which respectively held the Italian records for the number of enemy vessels and tonnage sunk.
- <u>RK awarded</u>: posthumously 26 May 1943
- K.I.A. Atlantic Ocean, 23 May 1943, 300 km SW of Cape Finisterre by a bomber from the British destroyer *"Active"* when in command of submarine *"Leonardo da Vinci"*
- After WW2 two submarines were named after him, the first a USN submarine originally named *"Volador"* which was built at the Portsmouth Naval Yard in Maine and entered service on 1 October 1948, but was later transferred to the Italian navy. The second was the Italian built *"S525"*.

Capitano di Fregata Enzo Grossi after receiving his Knight's Cross from Admiral Karl Dönitz.

Grossi, Enzo

- <u>Born</u>: San Epigma (Brazil), 20 April 1908
- <u>Rank at time of award</u>: Lieutenant Colonel (Capitano di Fregata)
- <u>Command at time of award</u>: Captain of submarine *"Barbarigo"*
- <u>RK awarded</u>: 7 October 1942 after he claimed to have sunk one Maryland and one Mississippi class USN battleships on 20 May and 6 October 1942 respectively. These claims were later found in court to have been unfounded, he was stripped of his rank and demoted to infantry private and his awards withdrawn. But there are those who claim he was unfairly treated and that he did sink two important USN vessels, but possibly not of the class Grossi had claimed
- <u>Died</u>: Argentina, 11 August 1960

Martinat, Giulio

- <u>Born</u>: Maniglia di Perrero (Turin Province), 24 February 1881
- <u>Rank at time of award</u>: Brigadier General (Generale di Brigata)
- <u>Command at time of award</u>: Army Corps Chief of Staff (Capo di Stato Maggiore di Corpo d'Armata) and C.O. of the *"Edolo"* Alpini Battalion
- <u>RK awarded</u>: posthumously 3 April 1943
- K.I.A. 26 January 1943 Nikolayevka, Russian Front

Messe, Giovanni

- <u>Born</u>: Mesagne (Brindisi Province), 10 December 1883
- <u>Rank at time of award</u>: Lieutenant General (Generale di Corpo d'Armata)
- <u>Command at time of award</u>: G.O.C. Italian Expeditionary Corps in Russia (Corpo di Spedizione Italiano in Russia, or C.S.I.R.)
- <u>RK awarded</u>: 23 January 1942
- Died of natural causes in Rome, 18 December 1968

Generale di Brigata Giulio Martinat.

Generale Giovanni Messe.

Alessandro Pavolini.

Borghese in conversation with Tenente Colonnello Luigi Carallo.

It is noteworthy that all 9 of these recipients had been recommended for and awarded their RKs while Italy was still fighting on the German side, and therefore before the creation of the fascist Italian Social Republic (RSI) and the raising of its 600,000-man armed forces (September 1943 – April 1945). Going down another level, we come to the Iron Cross 1st Class, which we will abbreviate EK1. In fact, as will be seen below, this was the highest level of Iron Cross awarded to soldiers of the RSI's armed forces, although and not surprisingly the vast majority received only the 2nd Class (EK2). Whilst the above details are available for the nine Italian recipients of the Knight's Cross, relatively little is known of those who were recommended for and then either awarded or denied the 1st and 2nd Class Iron Cross. The two best known recipients of the relatively humble EK2 were Minister **Alessandro Pavolini** and Capitano di Fregata Prince **Junio Valerio Borghese**, respectively the commanders of the infamous Black Brigades (Brigate Nere – formed by militarizing the Republican Fascist Party – PFR - on 1 July 1944) and the 10th Anti-Submarine Motor Boat Flottila (Xa Flottiglia MAS), both primarily engaged in anti-partisan warfare. Minister of Popular Culture (Ministro della Cultura Popolare, or MILCUPOP) and General Commander of the Black Brigades (Comandante Generale delle Brigate Nere) of the RSI, **Alessandro Pavolini** (born Florence 27 September 1903, executed 28 April 1945 at Dongo, Lake Como). Capitano di Fregata Principe **Junio Valerio Borghese** (born Artena, Rome Province, 6 June 1906 – 12 September 1943 signed a separate treaty of alliance with the *Kriegsmarine* – commander of the 10th Anti-Submarine Motor Boat Flottila (Xª Flottiglia MAS) during the RSI, died Cadiz, Spain, 26 August 1974).

Associazione Nazionale fra Decorati della Croce di Ferro

Of some interest and doubtless surprise to some of our readers is the fact that a "National

Association amongst those Decorated with the Iron Cross" (*Associazione Nazionale fra Decorati della Croce di Ferro*) was established in Venice in 1959.

Junio Valerio Borghese.

Observe of a membership card (*Tessera*) No. 9441 of the ANDCF.

ASSOCIAZIONE NAZIONALE FRA DECORATI DELLA CROCE DI FERRO

STATUTO

Art. 1 - E' costituita fra combattenti italiani decorati al Valor Militare con la CROCE DI FERRO, una Associazione Nazionale con Sede Centrale in Venezia e con Sezioni in Italia e all'Estero.

Essa si intitola: ASSOCIAZIONE NAZIONALE FRA DECORATI DELLA CROCE DI FERRO.

L'Associazione è apolitica, indipendente ed estranea all'attività di qualsiasi partito politico; essa riunisce quegli italiani che sui campi di battaglia abbiamo avuto tangibile riconoscimento del loro valor militare con la concessione della Croce di Ferro.

SCOPO

Art. 2 - Essa si propone:

a) - di custodire la memoria sacra dei Caduti per la Patria e tener desto l'orgoglio per gli atti di valore compiuti nel santo nome d'Italia.

b) - tutelare gli interessi materiali e morali dei Decorati e delle loro famiglie.

COMPONENTI

Art. 3 - Dell'Associazione possono far parte tutti i combattenti italiani che siano stati decorati al V. M. con la Croce di Ferro nei vari gradi, documentandone l'avvenuta concessione, purché si siano comportati e si comportino secondo le leggi dell'onor militare e della dignità personale, sia durante la vita militare che in quella civile.

Potranno inoltre far parte dell'Associazione anche i congiunti dei Caduti che furono decorati della Croce di Ferro.

PROVENTI

Art. 4 - I proventi dell'Associazione sono costituiti dalle quote sociali, doni, legati, rendite patrimoniali.

ASSEMBLEA

Art. 5 - L'assemblea dei Soci è il maggior organo responsabile dell'Associazione.

Essa si riunisce almeno una volta all'anno e, inoltre, a richiesta del Consiglio Direttivo o quando un quinto dei Soci lo domanda.

Essa è convocata dal Consiglio Direttivo.

L'Assemblea dà scarico al Consiglio della sua gestione annua ed al tesoriere per la tenuta dei conti annuali, fissa la quota annua sociale e decide sugli affari che non sono di pertinenza di altri organi sociali.

Le decisioni dell'Assemblea sono prese a maggioranza dei Soci presenti, ognuno di essi disponendo di un voto.

CONSIGLIO DIRETTIVO CENTRALE

Art. 6 - L'Associazione è diretta da un Consiglio composto da 5 membri designati, la prima volta, dall'assemblea costitutiva della Associazione, poi dalla maggioranza dei membri dell'Associazione in assemblea annuale o straordinaria.
Presidente, un Segretario Generale ed un Tesoriere.

Il Consiglio designa nel proprio seno un Presidente, un Vice-Il Consiglio Direttivo Centrale gestisce gli affari dell'Associazione, la rappresenta nei riguardi dei terzi e l'impegna validamente con la firma del Presidente, o in caso d'impedimento, del vice-presidente o di un membro del Consiglio.

Il Consiglio decide l'ammissione e l'esclusione dei Soci.

In caso di uguaglianza dei voti nell'assemblea o nel Consiglio Direttivo Centrale il voto del Presidente deciderà.

SEZIONI

Art. 7 - In ogni luogo dove si trovino almeno 5 decorati, in Italia o all'Estero, può essere costituita una sezione che si reggerà con le norme di cui agli art. 5 e 6 del presente Statuto, in quanto applicabili, e sarà presieduta da un Consiglio Direttivo Sezionale di 3 Soci.

SCIOGLIMENTO

Art. 8 - Lo scioglimento dell'Associazione può essere deciso o dal Consiglio Direttivo, all'unanimità dei suoi membri, o da una Assemblea generale straordinaria dei Soci, presenti almeno i due terzi di questi, su decisione dei tre quarti almeno dei Soci presenti.

Statutes of ANDCF.

Its declared aim was "*to safeguard the sacred memory of those who fell for the homeland and to keep awake the pride for the acts of valor performed in the sacred name of Italy, as well as to protect the material and moral interests of those who were decorated and their families*". The lawyer Avv. Umberto Corrado was the Association's National President (*Presidente Nazionale*), who chaired the Governing Council (Consiglio Direttivo). Membership was open to those who could prove they had been awarded an Iron Cross, be that 1st of 2nd Class and it is possible than one or more of the Knight's Cross Holders who survived the war may have joined the Association. Where 5 or more recipients got together, they could form Sections (*Sezioni*) of the Association, not only in Italy, but also abroad. The history and fate of the Association is not known (there is no record of it in Venice or elsewhere today) and it is not known whether EK recipients who fought on the German side during the Italian Social Republic from September 1943 to the end of the war were welcome or even admitted to the Association. In the late 1950s it is unlikely that former partisans (such as Trevisani – see below) would have looked kindly at joining an Association open to former soldiers of the RSI, let alone of the Italian SS, and such a view could have prevented such recipients from joining. Each member was issued with a numbered membership card (*tessera*), which showed on the obverse the rank and name of the holder (presumably at retirement, not when the EK was awarded), his town of residence and the class of Iron Cross he had been awarded, and had spaces on the reverse for annual renewal stamps. It is possible, but not yet confirmed, that Italian women, such as nurses and auxiliaries, were eligible for the EK and so should have been welcomed by this Association.

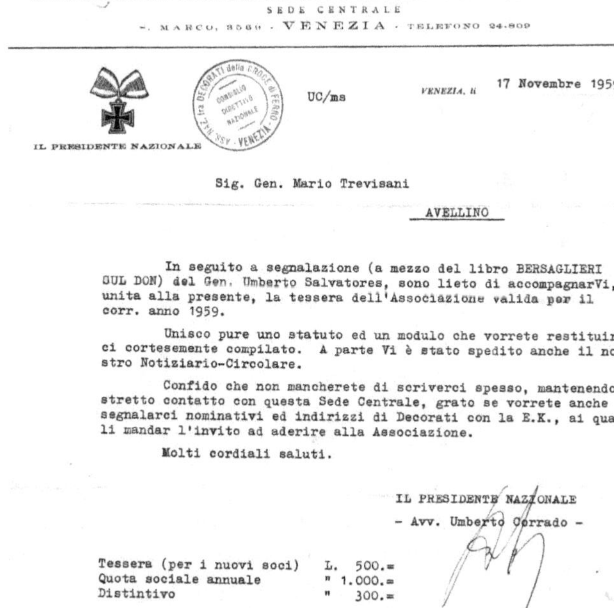

ASSOCIAZIONE NAZIONALE FRA DECORATI DELLA CROCE DI FERRO
SEDE CENTRALE
. MARCO, 3560 · VENEZIA · TELEFONO 24.800

UC/ms   VENEZIA, lì   17 Novembre 1959

IL PRESIDENTE NAZIONALE

Sig. Gen. Mario Trevisani

AVELLINO

In seguito a segnalazione (a mezzo del libro BERSAGLIERI SUL DON) del Gen. Umberto Salvatores, sono lieto di accompagnarVi, unita alla presente, la tessera dell'Associazione valida per il corr. anno 1959.

Unisco pure uno statuto ed un modulo che vorrete restituirci cortesemente compilato. A parte Vi è stato spedito anche il nostro Notiziario-Circolare.

Confido che non mancherete di scriverci spesso, mantenendo stretto contatto con questa Sede Centrale, grato se vorrete anche segnalarci nominativi ed indirizzi di Decorati con la E.K., ai quali mandar l'invito ad aderire alla Associazione.

Molti cordiali saluti.

IL PRESIDENTE NAZIONALE
- Avv. Umberto Corrado -

Tessera (per i nuovi soci)   L.   500.=
Quota sociale annuale   " 1.000.=
Distintivo   "   300.=

Letter from the National President of the ANDCF, Avv. (= lawyer) Umberto Corrado, to General Mario Trevisani, inviting him to join the Association and attaching a membership card, statutes and membership application form. Dated 17 November 1959, the letter explains that it was written after Trevisani's name had been found in the book "Bersaglieri sul Don" ("Sharpshooters on the Don") by General Umberto Salvatores and announced that the Association's newsletter was being sent to him under separate cover. It ends with an appeal for the names and addresses of any recipients of the Iron Cross Trevisani may have known, so they could be contacted and invited to join the Association. The costs of membership are also shown: Lire 500 (US$ 0.80 at that time) for a membership card of a new member (thereby confirming that renewal was intended to be a stamp on the back of the card, and not by issue of a fresh tessera), Lire 1,000 (US$ 1.60) annual dues and Lire 300 (US$ 0.53) for the Association's badge – the design of the badge is not known, but likely included the EK2 on its ribbon that appears on the Association's headed letter paper. Mario Trevisani was born on 7 July 1894, was commissioned into the Italian Army on 25 December 1916 and was promoted to "First Captain" (Primo Capitano) on 1 December 1926 and subsequently reached the rank of Colonel in the Bersaglieri (Sharpshooters). He fought on the Russian front but sided with the Allies after Italy turned against the Germans in September 1943 and went on to command the "Partisan District Command" (Comando Piazza Partigiano) in Bologna until early April 1945, when he was chosen to lead the local partisan brigades in a formation that was to be known as the Bologna Division of the Volunteer Corps for Liberty (Divisione Bologna del Corpo Volontario della Libertà). This formation was instructed to wait for the imminent Allied attack on Bologna and then, when the secret signal was given, to attack pre-determined

German positions. But as it turned out, the Germans abandoned the city during the night of 20/21 April 1945 and so Bologna was liberated early the next morning without a shot being fired by Allied units of the 20th Polish Corps *of the* British 8th Army, *of the 34th and 91st US Infantry Divisions and the* "Legnano", "Friuli" *and* "Folgore" *battle groups of the* "Maiella" *Partisan Brigade. Trevisani retired with the rank of General.*

Whilst we do not know, and will probably never find out, the number of Italians who were awarded the Iron Cross, it is interesting to note that the card illustrated in this article was numbered 9441. Now this may seem extraordinarily high, but it does not necessarily mean that there were at least 9,441 awards: such was the number of a card sent to a potential member in November 1959, and apart from the fact that he, as others, may have preferred not to join the Association, it is also possible that the first card issued was not numbered 1, so as to give the false impression that the Association had more members than was in fact the case. This author has spent little time recording details of Italian recipients of the Iron Cross, other than those of the Italian SS. These are listed below, although this must be considered as incomplete and so the author and publisher would appreciate details of other recipients to allow us to add to our database and, if justified, follow up with an eventual updated and ideally expanded version of this article.

ATTIMENTO

NOSTRI LEGIONARI
decorati e promossi

Sono stati insigniti della Croce di Ferro di II classe

S. Ten. SS Flick *Massimo*, di Torino.
Serg. SS Orlandoni Pietro, di Castel S. Giovanni (Piacenza).
Serg. SS Grandi Giovanni, di Gudo Visconti (Milano).
Serg. SS Fiaschi Oceanico, di Rosignano Marittimo (Livorno).
Leg. SS Mascitti Ermenegildo, di Milano.

Sono stati promossi di grado per merito di guerra

Leg. SS Gatti Enrico, di Milano, promosso caporale.
Leg. SS Magnani Alfiero, di Chiaravalle (Ancona), promosso caporale.
Cap. SS Menghini Guglielmo, di Castelnuovo Abate (Montalcino - Siena), promosso caporal maggiore.
Leg. SS Biglino Aldo, di Torino, promosso caporale.
Leg. SS Italiani Giuseppe, di Pesaro, promosso caporale.
Leg. SS Corticelli Leandro, di Cernobbio (Como), promosso caporale.
Leg. SS Consonni Felice, di Meda (Milano), promosso caporale.

Sono stati insigniti del distintivo d'onore di feriti

Cap. Magg. SS Caprino Antonio, di S. Fradello (Messina).
Cap. Magg. SS Loreggia Angiolo, di Venezia.
Cap. Magg. SS Cullotta Giovanni, di Lipari (Messina).
Leg. SS Valenti Salvatore, di Messina.
Leg. SS Motta Fiorentino, di Gropello d'Adda (Milano).

The names of 5 recipients of the EK2 belonging to the Italian SS Legion are listed in "*Avanguardia*", 6 May 1944.

Italian SS recipients of the Iron Cross

Given the author's specific research into the Italian SS over 40 years it is possible to provide a list of at least some of those who were awarded the Iron Cross. This number, 40 at the last count, is almost certainly incomplete, given that in December 1944 the Italian SS newspaper "*Avanguardia*" reported that no less than 44 Iron Crosses had been awarded to the men of just one battalion and its commander *Waffen-Standartenführer* Carlo Federigo degli Oddi, for their bravery in action against US troops on the Anzio/Nettuno breachhead between March and the beginning of June 1944, that is the IInd Battalion (known also as both "*Degli Oddi*" after its commander and "*Vendetta*", meaning "Revenge") of the 1st Infantry Regiment of what the Italians knew at that time as the "*1ª Brigata italiana granatieri armati della SS*", literally "1st Italian Armed Grenadiers Brigade of the SS"(4).

Sketch of the field award of the first 5 EK2s to men of the Italian SS by the popular illustrator Gino Boccasile (born Bari, 14 July 1914, contributed cartoons and sketches to "*Avanguardia*", designed the 3 best-known recruiting posters for the Italian SS; by 14 March 1945 a *Sonderführer* (Z) in the Italian SS Legion's Press and Propaganda Department (Abteilung Presse und Propaganda (*Einheiten d. Ital Waffenverbände der SS*)); died Milan, 10 May 1952).

That Italian SS soldiers had been awarded the EK2 was first announced at the end of April 1944, when the news that 5 members of the Italian SS Legion – including a 17-year-old – was published in the Italian SS newspaper "*Avanguardia*"[5]. The names were not included in this first announcement, but were published on 6 May 1944 in the following issue[6] and were Fiaschi, Flick, Grandi, Mascitti and Orlandoni. The Germans were not in the habit of complimenting members of the Italian armed forces, especially after the despised volte-face of 8 September 1943, but an exception was made on 28 April 1944 when *SS-Oberführer* Prof. Karl Diebitsch, who since March of that year had commanded a Battle Group that included Italian SS on the Anzio/Nettuno front and would do so until early June, was so impressed with the bravery of 7 members of the "*Degli Oddi*" SS Battalion under his command that he put pen to paper and informed no less than Benito Mussolini himself that they had been awarded the EK2.

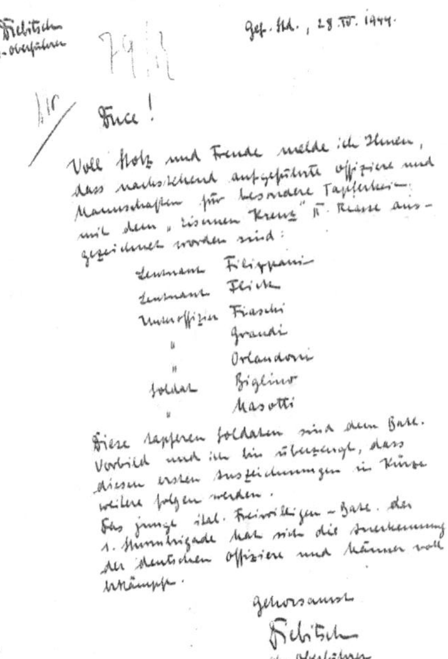

Letter to Mussolini from SS-Oberführer Karl Diebitsch of 28 April 1944, which reads in literal translation: "Duce! (With) the maximum of pride and joy I inform you that the officers and soldiers listed below have been decorated with the Iron Cross 2nd Class: Leutnant Filippani, Leutnant Flick, Unteroffizier Fiaschi, Unteroffizier Grandi, Unteroffizier Orlandoni, Soldat Biglino, Soldat Mascitti. These courageous soldiers are an example to the battalion and I am convinced that these first decorations will soon be followed by others. The young battalion of Italian volunteers of the 1st Assault Brigade (1. Sturmbrigade) deserves recognition by the German officers and soldiers". It is noteworthy that Diebitsch used German army ranks, not those of the Waffen-SS.

Sketch of *SS-Oberführer* Prof. Karl Diebitsch published in *"Avanguardia"*.

I nostri decorati

Dal fronte di Nettuno giunge la notizia che altri dieci volontari della Legione SS Italiana sono stati decorati sul campo della Croce di Ferro di II Classe. Vengono segnalate anche alcune promozioni per merito di guerra.

Un altro reparto SS in linea

Da alcuni giorni un nuovo reparto della Legione SS Italiana è giunto sul fronte di Nettuno. Alla prova del fuoco i nuovi arrivati si sono dimostrati degni dei commilitoni che li hanno preceduti.

Per i nostri feriti

Sulle rive del Lago Maggiore è stata scelta una magnifica residenza, dove passeranno la licenza di convalescenza i nostri valorosi feriti.

Under the heading *"Those of us who have been decorated"*, in the 13 May 1944 issue of *"Avanguardia"* it was reported that *"News has arrived from the Nettuno front that another 10 volunteers of the Italian SS Legion have been decorated on the field with the IInd Class Iron Cross. A number of field promotions for war merit are also advised"*.

These were the 5 already mentioned above and two others: *Leutnant* Filippani (in fact Filippani-Ronconi) who had actually been the first to receive the award five days after he had been severely wounded on 14 April 1944 - so it is difficult to understand why he had not been mentioned before - and Soldat Biglino who, together with Filippani-Ronconi, had to wait until August 1944 to physically receive their Crosses.

News that a further 10 EK2s had been awarded to Italian SS men fighting at Nettuno followed on 13 May 1944[7], but this appears to have been corrected a week later in the next issue of *"Avanguardia"*[8], which referred to 12 EK2s being awarded, 4 personally by Maresciallo Graziani.

After what was courageous and bloody genuine front line action against vastly superior US forces at Anzio and Nettuno, the elements of the Italian SS were engaged almost entirely in less glorious if not infamous anti-partisan warfare and degli Oddi commanded a battle group (*SS-Kampfgruppe*) that took on partisans in Val Pellice and Chisone in August 1944 in Operation *"Nachtigall"*.

An impressive ceremony was held at Mariano Comense on 23 November 1944, when Graziani awarded the prestigious Italian Silver Medal of Military Valor (Medaglia d'Argento al Valor Militare) to the IInd Battalion of what had by then been renamed from Infanterie-Regiment 1 of the Italian SS Brigade to *Waffen-Grenadier-Regiment der SS 81*, and "numerous" more Iron Crosses were awarded to men of *"Italian and German elements of the SS Brigade"* (1ª Brigata italiana granatieri armati della SS, in particular its IInd Battalion, 1st SS Regiment), including Colonnello degli Oddi the former C.O. of

RICONOSCIMENTO D'ONORE

Il Comandante Supremo della SS, Reichsfuehrer Heinrich Himmler, quale riconoscimento per le dimostrazioni di valore e di senso del dovere dei volontari della Legione SS Italiana, ha diramato in data 3 maggio il seguente ordine:

« I reparti costituiti o da costituire in Italia, in quanto non si tratti di formazioni di polizia, sono considerati reparti della SS con tutti i doveri e con tutti i diritti ».

Il sangue e la vita dei nostri valorosi commilitoni schierati sul fronte di Nettuno, hanno guadagnato alla Legione questo altissimo riconoscimento. La parità di doveri e di diritti coi camerati della SS germanica costituisce il più alto onore e la più grande dimostrazione di fiducia che potevamo attenderci. Essa impegna tutti i comandanti e gli uomini al più alto rendimento.

RICOMPENSE AL VALORE

Un corriere dal fronte di Nettuno annuncia che, nel corso degli ultimi combattimenti, sono state conferite 12 Croci di Ferro ai nostri volontari. Il Maresciallo Graziani ha presenziato alla consegna di alcune di esse. Una cinquantina di legionari sono stati promossi per merito di guerra al grado superiore.

This item in "Avanguardia", published on 20 May 1944, reports how "a messenger from the Nettuno front has reported that, in the course of the latest combat, 12 Iron Crosses have been awarded to our volunteers. Marshal Graziano was present at the award of some of these. About 50 volunteers were promoted to the next rank up for war merit".

Waffen-Grenadier **Giuseppe Vassalli.**

the *"Vendetta"* Battalion and Capitano Fischetti who had also served at Nettuno and commanded that Battalion's 2nd Company. Curiously, it is reported that this brought the total of Iron Crosses awarded to men of the *"Degli Oddi"* Battalion for their bravery on the Anzio/Nettuno front to 20, when – as has been seen above – in the 30 December 1944 issue of *"Avanguardia"* it was to be reported that the total was more than double, 44. It is possible, therefore, that 20 had been awarded for action at Anzio/Nettuno in what was a rare and genuine example of front line combat by RSI troops against Allied forces, and a further 22 for action that followed further north against partisans, especially in Piedmont. It is perhaps significant that today, 70 years on, there are 22 EK2s on the standard of the old comrades' and supporters' association of the 29th SS Division: could this be that they prefer to honor their genuine front line service, and ignore – if not conceal - their highly criticized and far less savory deeds against their partisan fellow countrymen, then referred to as *"the rebels"*? Veteran of the IInd Battailon, 82nd Regiment of the 29th SS Division, *Waffen-Grenadier* Giuseppe Vassalli, was unable to explain to the author in Milan in May 2015 why 22 EK2s had been added to the banner of his Association, adding only that he had found that to have been the number awarded to members of the *"Degli Oddi"* Battalion who had fought at Anzio/Nettuno, *"in a book"*…

It is interesting to note that although degli Oddi had been recommended for the EK2 for his actions at Anzio/Nettuno four months previously, he only received the award at the Mariano Comense ceremony, as the original documentation in support of the award had been lost, and the subsequent recommendation was for this and his anti-partisan actions in Operation *"Nachtigall"*.

SS-Obergruppenführer und General der Waffen-SS Karl Wolff, the Highest SS and Police Leader in Italy (*Der Höchste SS- und Polizeiführer in Italien*), pins an EK2 on the chest of a *Waffen-Untersturmführer* of the former *"Degli Oddi"* Battalion at Mariano Comense, 23 November 1944.

While in the background *SS-Gruppenführer und Generalmajor der Waffen-SS* Lothar Debes, the *Waffen-SS* commander in Italy (*Befehlshaber der Waffen-SS in Italien*), looks elsewhere, Wolff pins an EK2 on the chest of an Italian SS private at Mariano Comense on 23 November 1944.

Other officers to receive the EK2 on 23 November 1944 were *Waffen-Hauptsturmführer* Lorenzo Fischetti, who had commanded the 2nd Company of degli Oddi's Battalion at Anzio/Nettuno, and *Waffen-Sturmbannführer* Martinelli, easily recognizable by over-size black SS runes painted on the side of his Italian steel helmet, who had led the anti-tank unit of the Italian SS Brigade (*Pak-Abt. WGB-SS (Ital. Nr.1)*) in action against partisans.

Left photo, standard (labaro in Italian, from the Latin labarum) of the veterans' and supporters' Association of the 29th Division of the *Waffen-SS* (Italian No.1), on the occasion of the 70th anniversary celebrations of the sacrifice of the men and women of the armed forces of the Italian Social Republic, who fell fighting with the Germans from 9 September 1943 to the end of the war in Italy. The photograph was taken at 10:30AM on the morning of 26 April 2015 at Field Ten of the Masocco cemetery in Milan. It is to be noted that 22 EK2s are attached to the standard, corresponding approximately to the number awarded to men of the *"Degli Oddi"* Battalion who fought the US Army at Anzio and Nettuno between March and June 1944. This suggests they do not take into consideration the other EK2s that the men of that same Battalion were later awarded for action against Italian partisans. **Right photo**, The standard of the veterans' and supporters' Association of the 29th Italian SS Division, photographed by the author at the Association's stand at *"Militalia"*, Novegro (Milan), 16 May 2015.

Left: The Association's standard without the Iron Crosses. Right, the Association's pennant *II.Btl.*

SS-Oberführer **Erich Tschimpke inspecting Italian SS soldiers.**

Legionario SS Arturo Albenga (Photograph by war correspondent Renzi, published in the illustrated magazine *"Sveglia"*, number 5, 8 December 1944).

In listing the Italian SS recipients of the EK below we have shown, where possible, the position, rank and unit that were valid at the time the action or actions were performed that warranted recommendation for and award of the EK. The ranks are those found in documents, which are either Italian army or those of the German *Waffen-SS* or army. The following abbreviations are used for the units:

Abt.= Abteilung (battalion – e.g. anti-tank)
Btl.= Bataillon (battalion – e.g. infantry)
Freiw.= Freiwilligen (volunteer)
IR= Infanterie-Regiment (infantry regiment)
Ital.= italienische (Italian)
KG= Kampfgruppe (battle group)
Kp.= Kompanie (company)
MG= Machinengewehr (machine gun)
Pak.= Panzerabwehrkannone (anti-tank)
Rgt.= Regiment (regiment)
Sq.= Squadra (squad)
WGB=Waffen-Grenadier-Brigade (infantry brigade)
WGR=Waffen-Grenadier-Regiment (infantry regiment)
zbV= zur besonderen Verwendung (special purpose)
Zg.= Zug (platoon)

Although 7 of the 17 known recommendations for award of the EK2 for action against partisans were in fact denied, they have been included below for the sake of interest and completeness.

ALBENGA, Arturo

<u>Born</u>: 19 May 1925, place unknown
SS-Sturmmann/Grenadier/Legionario SS
EK2 awarded May 1944 with effect from 20 September 1944 for his actions against Sherman tanks between Canale Mussolini and Borgo Podgora on the Anzio/Nettuno front (where he was captured but managed to escape US captivity)
<u>Unit</u>: 1. (also reported as 3.) Kp. Btg. *"Vendetta"* (a.k.a. II. Btl. *"Degli Oddi"*)/IR 1
Killed by partisans at the end of July 1944 at Garessio while on leave

ANATO, Arturo

<u>Born</u>: Ascoli Piceno, 4 May 1920
<u>Rank</u>: *Obergefreiter*
Recommendation for award of the EK2 for action

Italian SS volunteers in training, 1944.

Rank: *Waffen-Standartenführer/Oberst*
EK2 awarded with effect from 15 October 1944 for action as C.O. of KG 2 in action against partisans in Operation *"Nachtigall"* in the summer of 1944 in the area of Val Chisone and Roreto. The Cross was presented formally on 23 November 1944 at Mariano Comense.
Command/Unit: C.O. *KG 2/Stab IR 2*

CHIERICI, Loris

Born: Date and place not known
Rank: Waffen-Rottenführer
EK2 awarded prior to 15 May 1944 for action on the Anzio/Nettuno front
Unit: *II. Btl.* (= Battaglione *"Degli Oddi"*)/1 IR

COCO, Salvatore

Born: Date and place unknown
Rank: *Waffen-Scharführer/Waffen-Oberscharführer*/Sergente/Maresciallo
EK2 awarded 28 April 1944 for action on the Anzio/Nettuno front March/June 1944 and he was mentioned in *SS-Oberführer* Karl Diebitsch's order of the day of 13 May 1944
Unit: *3. Kp., II. Btl.* (= Battaglione *"Degli Oddi"*)/1 IR

COMINI, Aldo

Born: Nave (Brescia Province), 10 March 1914
Rank: *W-Hauptsturmführer/Hauptmann*
After commanding a company between February and May 1944 on the Nettuno front, he was recommended for the EK2 when in August 1944 in *II./IR 1* in action against partisans in the Ripa Valley, but this was denied on 31 October 1944
Unit: *II. Btl.*(= Battaglione *"Degli Oddi"*)/IR 1

CORTICELLI, Leonardo

Born: Cernobbio (Como), 5 July 1921
Rank: Legionario SS/caporale SS/*SS-Rottenführer/Gefreiter*
EK2 awarded with effect from 20 September 1944 for action on the Anzio/Nettuno front, 9 April 1944

Carlo Federico degli Oddi.

Sketch of Tenente Colonello (*W-Sturmbannführer*) degli Oddi, published in *"Avanguardia"*.

Unit: *II. Btl. (= Battaglione "Degli Oddi")/IR 1*

DAL DOSSO, Arturo

Born: Lavagno (Verona Province), 3 March 1896

Rank: *Hauptmann/W-Hauptsturmführer*

EK2 awarded with effect from 1 December 1944 following recommendation made on 18 November 1944, for action at the Anzio/Nettuno bridgehead in June 1944, and then against partisans in August 1944 in Operation *"Strassburg"* near Pessinetto and later in September/October 1944 in Operation *"Avanti"* near Bettola in the Piacenza province

Command/Unit: C.O. 2. *Kp., I. Btl. "Debica"/IR 1/WGB (ital. Nr. 1)*

DEGLI ODDI, Carlo Federico

Born Alexandria (Egypt), 3 February 1895

Rank: *Oberstleutnant*/Tenente Colonnello/*Waffen-Obersturmbannführer*

Proposed for the EK2 in June 1944 for his actions at Anzio/Nettuno, but not granted as the supporting documentation had been lost and he had to wait until 23 November 1944 to formally receive the award at Mariano Comense for his actions in August 1944 when commanding KG 1 against partisans in Operation *"Nachtigall"* in the Val Pellice and Chisone area in the summer of 1944. The Cross was formally presented on 23 November 1944 at Mariano Comense.

Command/Unit: C.O. *KG 1, II. Btl., IR 1*

DELLA VALLE, Luigi

Born: Alvanova (Naples Province), 16 May 1921

Rank: Legionario SS

Recommended for EK on 22 November 1944 for action against partisans on 30 September 1944 at Cuorgné in the Canavesano area when he killed the partisan leader Giuseppe Trione, known as *"Spartacus"* ("Spartaco" in Italian)

Unit: *WGB SS – Pak Abt. – II. 47/32 Zg.*

ESPOSITO, Gennaro[9]

Born: Naples, date unknown

Rank: *Sturmmann*/Legionario SS

EK2 awarded for action in patrols on the Anzio/Nettuno when he took 7 US soldiers prisoner and suffered 5 bullet wounds

Bruno Fattori (*Archivio Corbatti*).

Pio Filippani-Ronconi wears the EK2 ribbon in the second button hole of his *Waffen-SS* tunic.

Unit: *II. Btl.* (= Battaglione *"Degli Oddi"*)/IR 1[10]

Died: Belvedere Marittima (Cosenza Province), 1970

FATTORI, Bruno

Born: Date and place not known

Rank: *Unterscharführer*

EK2 awarded for action on the Anzio/Nettuno front March/June 1944

Unit: *II. Btl.*(Battaglione *"Degli Oddi"*)/1 IR

FERRARESE, Dante

Born: Venice, 7 July 1919

Rank: *Waffen-Obersturmführer / Oberleutnant*

Recommended for EK on 27 October 1944 for action at Nettuno in early June 1944 and then against partisans in June and near Turin in September 1944

Command/Unit: C.O. Zg. in *I. Btl. "Debica"* of *KG "Noweck"*, WGB SS (*ital. Nr. 1)/IR.1*(11)

FIASCHI, Oceanico

Born: Rosignano Marittimo (Livorno Province), date unknown

Rank: *Unterscharführer*/Sergente SS

EK2 awarded (one of the first 7) in the field on the Anzio/Nettuno front in April 1944; Mussolini was informed of the award by letter of 28 April 1944

Unit: *II. Btl.* (Batt. *"Degli Oddi"*)/1 IR

FILIPPANI-RONCONI, Pio

Born: Madrid (Spain) 10 March 1920

Rank: *SS-Untersturmführer* (not *Waffen-Untersturmführer*)/Oberleutnant/Tenente

EK2 awarded (the first of the first 5) on 19 April 1944 for action on the Anzio/Nettuno front where he was severely wounded, and Mussolini was informed by letter of 28 April. Presentation of the award had to wait until August 1944.

IM NAMEN DES FÜHRERS
VERLEIHE ICH
DEM

ϟϟ - Untersturmführer Pio Filippani-Ronconi

ϟϟ - Batl. Italia

DAS
EISERNE KREUZ
2. KLASSE

Div.Gef.St. 19. April 1944

(DIENSTSIEGEL)

Hildebrandt,

Generalmajor u. Kommandeur
der 715.Jnf.Div.(mot)
(DIENSTGRAD UND DIENSTSTELLUNG)

Award document for Filippani-Ronconi's EK2, signed at the HQ of the 715. *Infanterie-Division (mot.)* by its commander, 19 April 1944. To be noted: a) although Italian, the recipient's rank is given as if he were German ("*SS-*" rather than "*Waffen-*"), and b) his unit is shown generically and inaccurately as "*SS Battalion Italy*" (SS-Batl. Italia).

Italian SS volunteers in training, 1944.

Unit: *3. Zg, 1. Kp., II. Btl. (= "Degli Oddi"/"Vendetta"), 1 IR*
Died: Rome, 11 February 2010

FISCHETTI, Enzo[12]

Born: Catania, 12 November 1910
Rank: *Waffen-Hauptsturmführer/Hauptmann*
EK2 awarded for action in May 1944 on the Anzio/Nettuno front with effect from 20 September 1944
Command/Unit: *C.O. 2. Kp., II. Btl. /IR 1*

FLICK, Massimo

Born: Turin, date not known
Rank: *W-Untersturmführer*/Sottotenente SS
EK2 awarded (one of the first 5) on the Nettuno front for having driven off a patrol and then counter-attacking with just 4 men, killing 3 US soldiers and capturing a heavy machine gun in April 1944; Mussolini was informed of the award by letter of 28 April 1944
Command/Unit: *C.O. 1. Zg, 2. Kp., II. Btl. (= Battaglione "Degli Oddi")/IR 1*

FOIS, Giovanni

Born: 9 March 1918, place not known
Rank: *Obergefreiter*/Caporale
EK II awarded with effect from 20 September 1944, motivation unknown
Unit: *I.Btl. /IR 1*

FORMICA, Constantino

Born: Agazzino (Piacenza Province), 20 August 1916
Rank: *Soldat*
Recommendation for award of the EK2 for action against partisans near Colle del Lis in the Turin Province in August 1944 was denied on 31 October 1944
Unit: *II.Btl. /IR 1 WGB-SS (Ital. Nr. 1)*

GASPARI, Giovanni

Born: 9 February 1905, place not known
Rank: *Waffen-Oberscharführer/Feldwebel*
EK II awarded with effect from 20 September 1944 for action on the

A mortar from an Italian SS unit in action, 1944.

Karl Wolff awards *Waffen-Sturmbannführer* Pietro Martinelli the EK2 at Mariano Comense on 23 November 1944.

Anzio/Nettuno front March/June 1944
Command/Unit: C.O. 3. Zg, 2. Kp., II. Btl. (= Battaglione *"Degli Oddi"*)/1 IR 1

GRANDI, Giovanni

Born: Gudo Visconti (Milan Province), date unknown
Rank: Legionario SS – *Unterscharführer* - Sergente SS - Sergente Maggiore
EK2 (one of the first 5) awarded in the field in April 1944 on the Anzio/Nettuno bridgehead; Mussolini was informed of the award by letter of 28 April 1944; subsequently awarded the EK1 posthumously on 23 November 1944 for action against partisans.
Unit: *II. Btl.* (Batt. *"Degli Oddi"*)/1 IR
Killed by partisans 7 August 1944 at San Vito di Gaggiano (Milan Province) when on sick leave

GRONDINI, Alete[13]

Born: Date and place not known
Rank: Legionario SS/Soldato
Possibly awarded EK2 for action on Anzio/Nettuno beachhead
Unit: *II. Btl. /IR 1*

GULI, Stefano

Born: Genoa, 4 February 1920
Rank: *Waffen-Untersturmführer/Waffen-Obersturmführer*
EK2 awarded 23 November 1944 for action on 25 May 1944 on the Anzio/Nettuno front when he drove back 8 attacks by US troops
Command/Unit: C.O. 3. Zg, 1. Kp., II. Btl. (Battaglione *"Degli Oddi"*)/IR 1

MARTINELLI, Pietro

Born: Como, 2 September 1910
Rank: *W-Sturmbannführer / Hauptmann / Maggiore*
EK awarded effective 15 October 1944 for 3 actions against partisans in July and August 1944 when he commanded an SS

17-year old SS Legionnaire Ermengildo Mascitti from Milan, wearing the EK2 he won in April 1944 on the Anzio/Nettuno front. His uniform has no rank or other insignia, apart from a metal skull with a short sword between its teeth, as worn by the Black Brigades.

Walter Morini (*Archivio Morini*).

KG in operations at Colle del Lis (Turin Province) and in Operation "Bayreuth". He received the Cross from Karl Wolff on 23 November 1944 at Mariano Comense

Command/Unit: C.O. *Pak-Abt. WGB-SS (Ital. Nr. 1)*

MASCITTI, Ermenegildo

Born: Milan, 1927, day and month not known

Rank: Legionario SS/*Soldat*

EK2 (one of the first 5) and EK1 awarded in the field on the Anzio/Nettuno front in April 1944 for repeatedly going out on patrol and bringing back valuable intel; Mussolini was informed of the award by letter dated 28 April 1944.

Unit: *II.Btl. (= Battaglione "Degli Oddi"/"Vendetta")/IR 1*
Captured by US troops in late May 1944

MONETA, Nicola

Born: 31 August 1923, place not known

Rank: *Waffen-Unterscharführer / Obergefreiter* / Caporalmaggiore

EK2 awarded with effect from 20 September 1944 for action on the Anzio/Nettuno front in late April 1944 when, wounded, he managed to save a number of his wounded comrades from falling into American hands and, after hiding for three days, managed to get back to his unit

Unit: *II. Btl. (=Battaglione "Degli Oddi")/IR 1*

MORINI, Walter

Born: Reggio-Emilia, 27 June 1915

Rank: *Waffen-Oberscharführer* / SS Sergente Maggiore

EK2 awarded with effect from 1 December 1944, following recommendation made on 18 November

Members of the Italian SS Brigade.

An Italian SS soldier engaged in combat.

1944, for action at the Anzio/Nettuno bridgehead in June 1944, and then against partisans in September near Chiaves in Piedmont

Command/Unit: *Zg.*, *Btl. "Debica"*, *KG "Noweck"/ WGB ital.SS Nr. 1 I./IR 1*[14]

NEGRI, Francesco

Born: Vercelli, 3 June 1920
Rank: *Waffen-Unterscharführer*

EK2 awarded with effect from 1 December 1944 following recommendation made on 18 November 1944, for action at the Anzio/Nettuno bridgehead in June 1944, and then against partisans in September 1944 near Chialamberto in the Turin province

Command/Unit: *Sq.*, *Btl. "Debica"*, *KG "Noweck"/ WGB ital.Nr. 1 I./IR 1*[15]

NERONE, Amedeo

Born: 6 December 1912, place not known
Rank: *SS-Sturmmann/Grenadier*

EK2 awarded with effect from 20 September 1944 for action on the Anzio/Nettuno front March/June 1944

Unit: *II. Btl.* (= Battaglione *"Degli Oddi")/IR 1*

NICOLO, Antonino

Born: Reggio Calabria, 11 November 1922
Rank: Soldat

Recommendation for award of the EK2 for action against partisans at Fenestrelle in the Turin Province on 1 August 1944 when he was mortally wounded was denied on 31 October 1944

Unit: *I. Btl. /IR 2 WGB-SS (Ital. Nr. 1)*

OLIVOTTO, Emilio

Born: Nervesa Treviso (Treviso Province), 23 June 1921
Rank: *Schütze*

Sketches by Boccasile in *'Avanguardia'*.

EK2 awarded with effect from 15 October 1944 for action against partisans in August 1944 in the Susa Valley and presented at Mariano Comense on 23 November 1944

Unit: *Kp. zbV. WGB-SS (Ital. Nr. 1).*

ORLANDONI, Pietro

Born: Castel San Giovanni (Piacenza Province), date not known

Rank: *Waffen-Unterscharführer*/Sergente SS

EK2 (one of the first 5) awarded in April 1944 on the Anzio/Nettuno front for killing 5 soldiers of what was described at the time as the US "Kansas City" Division and driving off 28 others; Mussolini was informed of the award by letter dated 28 April 1944

Command/Unit: C.O. *1. Zg, 2. Kp., II. Btl.* (= Battaglione *"Degli Oddi"*)/IR 1

PIZZI, Roberto

Born: Stradella (Pavia Province), 26 March 1920

Rank: SS-Caporale Maggiore[15] / *Rottenführer*[16]

Recommended for EK2 posthumously on 5 May 1944 for action against partisans, having died from head wounds from a grenade on 21 March 1944 at Torre Pellice, Turin Province.

Unit: 1. Sturmbrigade Ital. Freiw. Legion

Died: K.I.A. 21 March 1944

RAGONI, Loy

Born: Poggi-Bonsi (Siena Province), 5 February 1921

Rank: *Unterscharführer*

Recommended for the EK2 on 5 May 1944 for action on 21 March 1944 at Torre Pellice (Turin Province), where he killed 4 enemy and was himself wounded.

Unit: *I. Btl./IR 1*

RATTI, Piero

Born: Milan, 29 November 1920

Rank: *Feldwebel*

Recommendation for award of the EK2 for action against partisans in early August 1944 was denied on 31 October 1944.

Tenente Davide Scano (*Archivio Scano*).

Italian SS soldiers, 1944.

Unit: *I. Btl. /IR 2 WGB-SS (Ital. Nr. 1)*

RIGO, Orazio

Born: Istrana (Treviso Province), 8 July 1921
Rank: *Waffen-Untersturmführer/Leutnant*
Recommended for EK2 on 27 October 1944, having served on the Anzio/Nettuno front and been engaged against partisans in August 1944 at Fenestrelle and in Operation *"Strassburg"*
Command/Unit: Zg., *Btl. "Debica", KG "Noweck"/WGB SS (ital. Nr. 1) I. Btl. /IR 1*[17]

SCANO, Davide

Born: 6 May 1900, place not known
Rank: *Waffen-Obersturmführer*/Tenente delle SS italiane
Awarded EK2 for action on Anzio/Nettuno front
Unit: Presumably *II. Btl.* (= Battaglione *"Degli Oddi"*)/IR 1, and by January 1945 he was Staff Officer of *81. WGRdSS of Brig.*
K.I.A. Mariano Comense, 28 April 1945

SOZZI, Aldo

Born: 1927, exact date and place not known
Rank: Legionario SS/Soldato
Recommended for EK2 for holding off superior US forces on 27/28 April 1944 on Anzio/Nettuno front, but such appears to have been denied[18]
Unit: *II.Btl.*(= Battaglione *"Degli Oddi"*) /IR 1

VOLPATO, Aldo

Born: Bari, 20 June 1920
Rank: *Waffen-Untersturmführer/Leutnant*
Recommended for EK2 on 27 October 1944 for action against partisans west of Turin in March 1944, on the Anzio/Nettuno front in June 1944, and against partisans in Operation *"Avanti"* in September/early October 1944
Unit: *I. Btl. "Debica"/IR 1/WGB SS (ital. Nr. 1)*

Endnotes

[1] Two sources have so far been found to suggest that an Italian air force fighter pilot, Francesco Panitteri di Lagarde (born in Genoa in 1921, died in Trapani, Sicily, 27 March 1990), was awarded the Knight's Cross in 1943. Wikipedia gives details of his birth and death and that he volunteered for the Italian Royal Air Force in 1939, became a pilot officer and early in WW2 was posted to the Trapani-Chinisia airport from whence he performed missions over Libya, Malta and the Balkans, clocking-up some 1,500 flying hours. In April 1942 he was shot down over Sicily and was given about a year to convalesce from wounds to one of his legs. He then served as

Secretary to the Fascist leader (Federale) in Trapani, Enzo Savorgnan di Brazzà, interrupting these duties to fly more missions. Prior to Mussolini's arrest and the fall of fascism on 25 July 1943 he had been denied authorization to fly in the Royal Air Force, which led him to apply to the Germans to allow him to serve in the *Luftwaffe*. After it became known on 8 September 1943 that Italy had changed sides against the Germans, he joined the Italian Social Republic and was invited by Enzo Savorgnan to take up a post as an official of the Republican Fascist Party in Reggio Emilia. He served as public prosecutor for the special extraordinary tribunal and during the course of one of the trials on 30 January 1944 he sought the death penalty for the priest Don Pasquino Borghi and eight other partisans and so was a party to the sentencing to death by firing squad of these men. In 1945 he became a pilot in the *Luftwaffe*, survived the war and joined the French Foreign Legion. Panitteri's son, Agostino, protested in July 2011 against the defamatory entries on Wikipedia in response to postings on the Italian forum of GAVS (Group of Friends of Historical Aircraft), claiming that his father's career was *"clear and honored"* and challenging anyone to prove otherwise. In his final post he accepted that his father had stood trial and had in fact been found guilty in the proceedings of first instance, but completely exonerated at appeal. This author wrote to Agostino Panitteri in June 2015, seeking confirmation that his father had indeed been awarded the Knight's Cross of the Iron Cross. He replied that this was indeed the case, and the award had been recommended by Albert Kesselring, who had previously awarded his father the EK1. But when asked to provide such basic details as when the recommendation had been made, when the award had been confirmed and presented, and the motivation for the award, the pilot's son declined to answer, having merely stated that he still had all of his father's medals and decorations at his home in Trapani.

[2] Although the spelling Di Giorgio is found in German sources (e.g. Gerhard von Seemen: *"Die Ritterkreuzträger 1939-1945"*, Verlag Hans-Henning Podzun, Bad Nauheim, 1955, p. 281 & Podzun-Verlag, Friedberg, 1976, p. 372 as well as Walther-Peer Fellgiebel: *"Die Träger des Ritterkreuzes des Eisernen Kreuzes 1939 – 1945"*, Podzun-Pallas, Friedberg/H, 1986, p.461), the correct spelling is Degiorgis and his year of birth was 1887 and not 1886: "Annuario Ufficiale delle Forze Armate del Regno d'Italia Anno 1936 – XIV I. Regio Esercito Volume I – Parte 1ª Ufficiali in Servizio Permanente e Personale Civile dell'Amministrazione della Guerra, N. 2946, Istituto Poligrafico dello Stato, Libreria, Roma, 1936 – Anno XIV, p. 75..

[3] The Turin daily *"La Stampa"* gave his first name as Federico in their death notice.

[4] *"Avanguardia. Settimanale della Legione SS Italiana"*, Anno I, N. 42, 30 dicembre 1944, p. 3. It is of interest to note that it was found necessary on 13 May 1944 to clarify that *"1. Sturmbrigade der italienischen freiw. Legion"* was identical to *Waffen-Grenadier-Brigade der SS (italienische Nr. 1)*, which on 27 April 1944 Himmler had ordered to be formed (*Tgb.nr roem 1a / 1628/44 geh., referring to fs. Nr. 5553 of 13 May 1944*)

[5] Ibid, Anno I, N. 7, 29 aprile 1944, p. 3

[6] Ibid, Anno I, N. 8, 6 maggio 1944, p. 3

[7] Ibid, Anno I, N. 9, 13 maggio 1944, p. 3

[8] Ibid, Anno I, N. 10, 20 maggio 1944, p. 3

[9] Giuseppe according to Corbatti/Nava, *"Sentire – Pensare – Volere. Storia della Legione SS italiana"*, Ritter, Milan, 2001, op.cit., p. 122

[10] Also found as *I. Bataillon.*

[11] SS-Pol.Rgt. 15, IIb 3300, O.U., den 27. Oktober 1944: "*Nachweisung über eingereichte Vorschläge auf Verleihung des EK. II. Klasse an italienische Wehrmachtangehörige*"

[12] Also found as Lorenzo

[13] According to Corbatti/Nava, op.cit., p. 106, the recommendation for Grondini's award was denied

[14] SS-Pol.-Rgt. 15 – O.U., den 18 November 1944: *Nachweisung über eingereichte Vorschläge auf Verleihung des Eisernen Kreuzes 2. Klasse.*

[15] *"Avanguardia - Settimanale della Legione SS Italiana"*, Anno I, N. 5, 15 aprile 1944

[16] *1.Sturmbrigade Ital. Freiw. Legion*, O.U., den 5. April 1944: *Vorschlagsliste Nr. 2 für die Verleihung des Eisernen Kreuzes II. Klasse, Der Kommandeur der 1. Sturmbrigade Ital. Freiw. Legion, i.V., SS-Oberführer* (signature illegible) *an den Höchsten SS-u.Pol.-Führer Italien.*

[17] SS-Pol.Rgt. 15, IIb 3300, O.U., den 27. Oktober 1944: "*Nachweisung über eingereichte Vorschläge auf Verleihung des EK. II. Klasse an italienische Wehrmachtangehörige*".

[18] According to Corbatti/Nava, op.cit., p. 104, the recommendation for Sozzi's award was denied.

Hitler's Cossacks

By Sergio Volpe

part 5

Cossack horsemen in the last months of the war.

A column of Cossack volunteers marching, Spring 1945.

Cossack volunteers dancing during a party.

Towards the end

On May 8, 1945, when the armistice was signed, two groups of Cossacks were stationed in southern Austria, not far from the border of the former Yugoslavia. A first group, made up of about 25,000 refugees, men, women and old people, militarily organized and led by Ataman Domanov, was located in the surroundings of Tolmezzo in Carniola. A second group, comprising the 18,000 soldiers of General von Pannwitz's 15th Cavalry Corps, was marching into southern Austria. In the first days of May, these two groups, still armed, for fear of being captured by the Soviet units or ending up in the hands of the Communist partisans, spontaneously surrendered to the British forces, hoping to escape the revenge of their enemies.

The Cossacks of the Ataman Domanov

As already mentioned above, the Cossacks of Don, Terek and Kuban, to escape the Red Army, were grouped by the Germans at the end of 1942 in Belarus, in the Novogrudok region. Thanks to the intervention of Ataman Pavlov, a very popular leader with an exceptional charisma, this heterogeneous mass of refugees quickly organized. Ruled according to Cossack traditions, this Cossack community in Belarus saw its

The Ataman Domanov, at left in the photo.

Cossack volunteers in Italy, Autumn 1944.

numbers swell with the arrival of large numbers of White Cossacks, including officers, who lived in exile in Western Europe. This community was equipped with a paramilitary defense corps (comprising four infantry regiments, two of the Don, one of the Terek and one of the Kuban), equipped with light weapons supplied by the Germans or taken from the Soviets. This corps was charged with assuming the defense of the colony against the communist partisans. On June 17, 1944, Ataman Pavlov was killed under mysterious circumstances in a suburb of the city of Novogrudok, possibly killed by a partisan. He was then replaced by Colonel Timotei Ivanovitch Domanov. Born in 1897, in the Cossack village of Migulinsk, Domanov served in the White armies of generals Kalédine, Krasnov and Denikin, with the rank of lieutenant. After the civil war, he lived in the Caucasus where he held administrative functions in numerous companies. On the eve of the Second World War, he settled in Piatigorsk, where he was placed in charge of the supply services of the local power plant. After the arrival of the Germans, he actively participated in the formation of Cossack units and became a recruiting officer in one of the regiments created by the Ataman Pavlov. Domanov had married a German-Ukrainian woman, a great organizer, who was fluent in German. It was under his influence and that of the German liaison officer, Hauptmann Müller, that Domanov was elected Ataman. In September 1944, with the Red Army approaching Minsk, the Germans decided to move the Cossack refugees to northern Italy. Under the direction of the ataman Domanov, the Cossacks resumed the march with their wheelbarrows, their horses, their cows and their dromedaries. After passing through Poland, Germany and Austria, they settled in Gemona in Friuli and then were assigned a provisional territory

Cossack volunteers with their families, 1944.

near Tolmezzo in Carniola. This community, according to British sources, numbered around 24,000 people, including women and children. In April 1945, the Cossacks were threatened by the advance of British troops and by the Italian partisans who exerted more and more intense pressure.

On April 27, three Italian officers met Domanov in his command post and asked the Cossacks to deliver all weapons and their evacuation from Italian territory. Domanov accepted only the second condition. The departure took place on April 28th. Domanov's intention was to cross the Austrian border via the Plöcken pass. At the head of the column, mounted units led the way, with Domanov's staff ahead. They were followed by an endless column of carts, laden with old men, women, the sick and children, preceded by the carriage of General Krasnov. As for Domanov, he waited with his bodyguard regiment for the return of a unit previously detached to Udine. Finally, a rearguard of several hundred Don and Terek Cossacks took up position south of Tolmezzo to repel any attacks by the partisans. And in fact, on more than one occasion, the Cossack column was attacked by the partisans. Bad weather conditions, rain and snow also slowed the column down. On the night of May 3, after crossing the Plöcken pass, the avant-garde arrived at Mauthe-Kötschach, the first Austrian village.

May 2, 1945: Cossack units retreating along the Büt valley towards the Plöckenpass.

Cossack units retreating towards the Plöckenpass.

Piotr Nikolajewitsch Krasnov.

On May 4, most of the units arrived in the Lienz sector. Once in Austria, the Cossack leaders consulted to decide what to do.

Krasnov was convinced that the commander-in-chief of the Allied forces in Italy, Harold Alexander, who had fought the Bolsheviks in Courland in 1919, would be sympathetic to the Cossacks. He then suggested that Domanov surrender to the British forces. A delegation, composed of General Leonide Vassilieff, the lieutenant Nicolai Krasnov (nephew of the general) and an interpreter, Olga Rotova, then went over the Plöcken pass and went to Tolmezzo. Here, he was received by General Robert Arbuthnott, commander of the 78th Infantry Division. During the interview, the British asked for the disarmament of the Cossacks, without however giving any real guarantee as to their fate. On May 5, General Musson, commander of the 36th Infantry Brigade, met with Domanov. The conversation was cordial. The British asked for the grouping of the Cossacks between Lienz and Oberdrauburg, along the Drava valley (Drau). The men would be allowed to keep their weapons up to the grouping area. In the second week of May, the Domanov Cossacks moved to the various temporary camps between Lienz and Oberdrauburg in the Drau valley. Domanov established his headquarters in Lienz. It should be noted that in this period, the Cossack leaders were unaware of all the agreements signed in Yalta, agreements that provided for

in World War Two 1939-1945

the surrender of all Soviet citizens who had fallen into the hands of the Allies at the end of the war. Krasnov also wrote a letter to Alexander, asking him to intervene on behalf of the Cossacks. On May 15, the Cossack camp was visited by the Red Cross, which distributed food and various effects. On May 17, Marshal Alexander telegraphed the British Army Chief of Staff in London to receive precise instructions regarding the Cossacks grouped in southern Austria, also specifying that any return to their country of origin would be fatal for their life. But it was not until May 29 that the British staff ordered Alexander to free the Cossacks. An order that came too late.

The Cossacks volunteers of the *1st Division* hand over their weapons to the British in the Feldkirchen sector, May 1945.

On May 18, General Arbuthnott visited the camp in Peggetz, not far from Lienz. At first he was cordial, then when Domanov pointed out that some horses had been taken away by the English soldiers, he replied: "There are no Cossack horses here. All the horses now belong to His Majesty the King of England whose Cossacks are the prisoners". Upon hearing the news of this altercation, Krasnov hastened to write to Alexander again. But again he received no response. Fate was now sealed and eventually all of Domanov's Cossacks were handed over to the Soviets. There were numerous cases of suicide, in order not to fall alive into the hands of the Bolsheviks. The others were all massacred in cold blood by the soldiers of the Red Army.

General Hellmuth von Pannwitz.

The fate of the Cossacks of the 15th Cavalry Corps

On May 8, 1945, von Pannwitz's Cossack cavalry corps still represented a considerable force, grouping around 20,000 men. These 20,000 men were divided into two large groups. After having managed to overcome a Bulgarian-Yugoslav barrage on the Drava, the 1st Cossack Division of Oberst Wagner, coming from Celje, had managed to take refuge in Austria, in an area about 80 kilometers east of Domanov's forces, between Völkemarkt and Wolfsberg. The 2nd Division and the General Staff of the Corps, pursued by the Bulgarian-Yugoslav forces, were still in Yugoslavia and were marching towards the Austrian border in the direction of Windisch-Feistritz. They then crossed the border in the night between 9 and 10 May. Meanwhile, General MacGreery's British 8th Army had arrived on the Italian-Austrian border. The British commander appointed an officer of the SOE (*Special Operations Executive*), Charles Villiers, to establish contact with the general staff of the 15th Corps. Villiers met Pannwitz and demanded the unconditional surrender of his units. Pannwitz agreed, but on the condition that his men would not be handed over to the Soviets. But Villiers replied that he had orders not to grant any conditions. In the following days, the various units surrendered to the English troops and were disarmed. When the news began to circulate that they would be handed over to the Soviets, many Cossack volunteers began, alone or in groups, to try to escape and together with them, the German personnel attached to the corps. On May 28, von Pannwitz and some German officers from his general staff were handed over to the Soviets at Judenburg. The rest of his men suffered the same fate. Fortunately, many, with the help of the English, managed to escape and thus avoid deportation and certain death. Von Pannwitz and the other officers of the Corps were tried and executed.

Bibliography

Massimiliano Afiero, "*I volontari stranieri di Hitler*", Ritter edizioni
Francois de Lannoy, "*Les cosacques de Pannwitz*", Editions Heimdal
D. Littlejohn, "*Foreign Legion of the Third Reich, Vol. 4*", R. Bender Publishing
Erich Kern, "*I Cosacchi di Hitler*", Ritter edizioni

TITOLI PUBBLICATI - ALREADY PUBLISHING

THE AXIS FORCES - NUMBER 1 - JANUARY 2017

THE AXIS FORCES - NUMBER 2 - APRIL 2017

THE AXIS FORCES - NUMBER 3 - JULY 2017

THE AXIS FORCES - NUMBER 4 - OCTOBER 2017

THE AXIS FORCES - NUMBER 5 - JANUARY 2018

THE AXIS FORCES - NUMBER 6 - APRIL 2018

THE AXIS FORCES - NUMBER 7 - JULY 2018

THE AXIS FORCES - NUMBER 8 - OCTOBER 2018

THE AXIS FORCES 9 - FEBRUARY 2019

THE AXIS FORCES 10 - MAY 2019

THE AXIS FORCES 11 - AUGUST 2019

THE AXIS FORCES 12 - DECEMBER 2019

THE AXIS FORCES 13 - FEBRUARY 2020

THE AXIS FORCES 14 - MAY 2020

WW2 AXIS
FORCES